τ

THE UNIVERSAL GRAVITY CODE

A Guide to Personal and Global Enlightenment

VIRGINIA ADAMS

THE UNIVERSAL GRAVITY CODE

A Guide to Personal and Global Enlightenment

Copyright © 2020 Virginia Adams. All rights reserved. No part of this publication may be reproduced, distributed, or transmitted in any form or by any means, including photocopying, recording, or other electronic or mechanical methods, without the prior written permission of the publisher, except in the case of brief quotations embodied in critical reviews and certain other noncommercial uses permitted by copyright law.

ISBN: 978-0-578-77021-5

Illustrations by Virginia Adams

Photography by Cyn Jones at Cynvision.com

Editing, Formatting and Cover Design by Transcendent Publishing

Virginia Adams and Virginia Adams Enterprises, Inc. make no promises, guarantees, representations and or warranties regarding medical diagnosis and or medical treatment, and are neither diagnosing, preventing, nor treating specific health challenges. You are solely responsible for your own medical care.

Printed in the United States of America.

DEDICATION

I dedicate this book to my grandchildren, Danny, Benjamin, Bodhi, Liliana, Isla, and Jade, and to all the youth on planet Earth. May you see only love, walk and talk in love, and transform our earth plane by "Being" Love. I see you, and I am honored to lead the way.

ACKNOWLEDGMENT

How do I begin to acknowledge the many beautiful souls who have touched my life and inspired me? I will name a few here, but know that if you are not listed it is not because your impact was not significant. My deepest love and appreciation goes out to my husband and children for their never-ending love and support. Immense gratitude goes to you, Marianne; you are my forever friend and cheerleader. I also want to thank Dr. Eric Pearl and all of my family at The Reconnection. Finally, to Kelly Simmons, your gentle eye and guidance as an editor gave me the strength and perseverance to push through the writing process.

CONTENTS

PREFACE vii
INTRODUCTION: Complex Stories, Simple Solutions xi
    The Term Gravity xii
    The Visions xii
        The Understanding xiv
        The Term "Know" xv
        The Many Names of God xv
PART I: Explore the Possibility 1
    CHAPTER ONE: What If 3
    CHAPTER TWO: Gloom and Doom 11
    CHAPTER THREE: The All Knowing Has Spoken 17
PART II: Embrace the Knowing:
What is the Gravity Code? 21
    CHAPTER FOUR: Seeds of Dis-ease:
    The Germination of the Code 23
    CHAPTER FIVE: The Endless Loop: Recognizing the
    Universal Gravity Code 27
    CHAPTER SIX: The Loop de Dupe 31
    CHAPTER SEVEN: Four Characteristics of a
    Gravity Code 37
PART III: Release the Illusion" Disarming the Gravity Code:
Rose-Colored Glasses 47
    CHAPTER EIGHT: It's Time to Wake up… NOW! 49

- CHAPTER NINE: Pi in the Sky 57
- CHAPTER TEN: The You Are Not Enough Bluff 61
- CHAPTER ELEVEN: Your True Self vs. Your Critic 69
- CHAPTER TWELVE: The Blame Game 73

PART IV: The Process: Dance of Freedom: The Components of Unconditional Love 79

- CHAPTER THIRTEEN: The Power of God 83
- CHAPTER FOURTEEN: The Truth of God 89
- CHAPTER FIFTEEN: The Love of God 93
- CHAPTER SIXTEEN: The Purity of God 97
- CHAPTER SEVENTEEN: The Wisdom of God 101
- CHAPTER EIGHTEEN: The Freedom of God 107
- CHAPTER NINETEEN: The Peace of God 111

CONCLUSION: Joy 119
EPILOGUE: The Grand Celebration 125
AUTHOR'S NOTES 127
ABOUT THE AUTHOR 133
BUT WAIT, THERE'S MORE! 135

PREFACE

Gazing out the window with sleepy eyes, I am mesmerized by the softly falling snowflakes. This is not what I anticipated seeing this morning as I was summoned awake by the triumphant aviary song of a new dawn. The vista before me provokes the feelings of early winter snowfall and the anticipation of the holiday season. But it is not December; it is April 17, 2020, and the unseasonable weather is just one more unanticipated event, albeit a lovely one, in a world that has been upended over the past few months. As I sip my morning tea and continue to gaze out the window, I realize that I am struggling to make sense of the stillness that my being is sensing. This snowy scene, the global virus of fear and the chaos of our current state of affairs, should have me feeling heavy and full of despair, and yet the only thing I sense or feel is peace and a vast stillness.

Looking back to last December, I recall being swept up in the excitement and anticipation of a new year. Each day in my morning meditation, I saw wildly vivid scenes of a new day dawning, and the idea of the year 2020 as being one of perfect vision spoke so elegantly to my inner knowing. I had said, written and lived the ideology of waking up, seeing past the veil of illusion, looking at our world and all of its chaos with a new perspective and using eyes of love to do so. Now 2020 became symbolic of these spiritual actions—the year of the awakening to our innate perfection through perfect "spiritual" vision. And five months later here we are, in the midst of the most significant global awakening ever known to man.

The global impact of the loss of income, loss of life, and loss of basic life comforts was not what I envisioned. I did not – could not – have imagined the screeching STOP to life as we knew it. In my wildest of dreams I did not see a time when we would collectively be asked, "Who am I if I can't color my hair, man- or woman-scape my body, hug my friends and family, go to the doctor with ease, get a massage, talk face-to-face with my accountant, go out to dinner, have a party, go to a concert, go on vacation, go to work, get a haircut, hold my grandbaby, visit my mother, go to church, celebrate my holy days, find f***ing toilet paper, sit in sacred circle, go on a retreat, pay my bills, have enough food to feed my family? Who am I if I lose my loved one?"

Has this been easy, NO!

Will things ever be the same again, NO!

Will we lose everything, MAYBE!

Will we lose a loved one, MAYBE!

Will my physical body die, YES!

Will I be the same me, YES!

Back to why I feel such a sense of tranquility this morning... I realize it is because I have wrestled with each of these questions my entire life, and I have already found peace.

My healing journey began with a search for methods to let go of fear. I had spent a lifetime riddled with fears, though as I would come to learn all of them were rooted in a fear of being me and seeing myself as a powerful divine being. As I pursued a fearless life, however, my eyes were opened to a new way of existence. Books that I had read before now seemed to have meaning; teachers who I had listened to before now began to make sense, and my meditations and self-awareness deepened.

One practice I found instrumental in peeling away my fear-based beliefs was journaling. What follows is an excerpt from an entry regarding love versus fear that I wrote when I was first beginning to accept that I am a healer:

What do I need and who do I need to tell me that I am enough? Why do I continue to hold on to things and ideas which are "fear-based," that tell me that I am not enough or that I am not special?

I sit here contemplating these papers, the messages, the cards … I understand that it was all a path. Everything has been a signpost – not badges, not magical emblems or words or symbols, just signpost to my innate abilities, and my perfection. We use cards, medicine, horoscopes, runes, fortune cookies, Ouija boards, et cetera to tell us who we are.

I will go out on a limb here and pretend that I am the all-knowing, the all-mighty see-er of all and tell myself that I AM CREATED IN THE PERFECTION OF MY SOURCE.

The only path, the only forward movement, the only relationship I need is with my higher self and my Source. Is that a narcissistic statement? No, it is the antithesis of a narcissist statement. When I connect to my Source, I connect to all others, because they are of the same Source. The only magic needed here is me saying YES to my Source and acknowledging my oneness to all.

In writing this, I realized that I AM THE MAGIC. WE ALL ARE. That is the essence of our innate healing power – knowing our connection to Source.

I let go of the idea that I am damaged, that I need to fix or repair myself and/or need to fix the perpetrators of my so-called damage. We heal ourselves, our families, and our world by seeing and emphasizing what we love and what is good; by seeing the perfection and magnificence in all, and most importantly, within ourselves. Only LOVE will save our souls, our lives, our nation, and our world. We make amends, we discover our wholeness of being, we align with the vibration of Source, and we become the frequency of LOVE.

As for the challenges we are facing now, well, this is gravity, folks. *God is gravity!* Not in the sense of punishment, but in the spirit of the gentle, kind demonstration that regardless of external circumstances, we are Love. Haven't we all, in one way or another, asked God, our Higher Power, to show us, to show us the way, to show me *Who am I and what is my purpose?* We call in whatever it will take to tear down the veil of illusion and open our eyes to perfect 20/20 vison. We even call in the grace – yes, the grace! – of grave times. And, as the outer world is figuratively or literally stripped away, with the grace of gravity, of God, we will see who we truly are. Sit in the quiet, sit in the stillness of nothingness, understand that you become the silent essence of peace without the chaos, without the need to proceed or do, the only thing left is the Knowing that you are still here, you still exist, and you are Love, and loved, despite of your hairy armpits.

Be well and know that I am always a phone call, text, IM, email, Marco Polo, Zoom video chat, telegram or telepathic message away. My lines are always open for authentic communication.

As always, I love you with all of my heart,

Virginia Adams
A Legacy of Love

INTRODUCTION

Complex Stories, Simple Solutions

You sometimes speak of gravity as essential and inherent to matter. Pray do not ascribe that notion to me, for the cause of gravity is what I do not pretend to know, and therefore would take more time to consider of it.

– Sir Isaac Newton

The Term Gravity

A normal everyday discussion with my husband planted the seed for this book. I don't recall exactly what we were talking about, but I do remember saying in a sarcastic tone, "Ah, the gravity of it ALL." In that moment I felt the correlation between the Earth's gravitational pull and the gravitational pull of our morose thoughts, or what my husband and I refer to as the "Human Condition." This realization came with an extreme rush of "Eureka!" which permeated every cell in my body. I instinctively knew that THIS WAS BIG!

The word gravity is commonly used to describe the gravitational pull of our solar system which keeps the planets in orbit. The Universal Law of Gravitation was a theory described through a mathematical equation introduced to us by Sir Isaac Newton and later expanded on by Albert Einstein.

According to this theory, gravity is what gives us weight, keeping us grounded and able to walk around without floating into the atmosphere.

I now propose that there is a similar "gravitational pull" – a program running simultaneously, whose sole purpose is to keep us grounded or focused on this earthly plane. This Universal Gravity Code is based on a different kind of equation and is one of disconnect and the participation in an illusionary world where "grave times" have our full attention. Once this code is detected and dismantled, there will be no limit to our ability to leave the illusions of this world and to gravitate to new levels of Love.

We may realize that we were actually meant to fly but have forgotten that we are trans-dimensional beings.

This idea has taken me on a wild exploratory excursion into the world of Sir Isaac Newton. As I explored, I began to see the human condition in quirky mathematical equations and a "what if" story regarding Isaac unfolded before me. Though whimsical in nature, I know there are aspects of TRUTH to this story. The more I dug into Isaac's life, the more I understood that we, the human race, have only been privy to a fraction of what he understood.

The Visions

Waking from a trancelike state, I looked down at my meditation notebook and saw these words scratched on the paper in almost indistinguishable lettering:

And the All that Is has spoken ...There are many laws governing our existence here in this realm. Be ye focused on the laws of the soul and turn your attention away from the laws of science, physics

INTRODUCTION

and nature. You have come to transform and enlighten your fellow travelers. Be about your work and bring the gifts of peace to others with your Divine Passion and Sweet essence.

Did I write that? I didn't remember interrupting my meditation to write anything. The only thing I knew was that my daily meditation had been exquisitely deep that morning. My day had started out the same as the previous three hundred-plus days: I rose at five a.m. and by five-forty-five I was seated in my healing space with a cup of tea, ready to resume my quest. I started my quiet time with the question I had been asking over and over again: *How do I disarm the Gravity Code?*

Somewhere at the end of 2017 or the beginning of 2018, I began hearing, seeing and sensing a presence that was asking me to look at the Universal Law of Gravity as it pertains to grave times. The awareness was coming in from all directions – relationships, teachings, clouds, and conversations – and I was being bombarded with information that was not of the sort I would usually look at.

During a morning meditation, I was shown the first vision of the whimsical "what if" scenario about Sir Isaac Newton's hidden life. This vision exposed the divine purpose of gravity and its evolutionary properties, revealing hidden secrets regarding our planet's future and our personal enlightenment. I was then told to write the story and a description of how the Universal Gravity Code was manifesting in our lives and society. I finished that work in a few intense writing days, when every word was given to me. I had become a scribe for the presence.

Since that initial "download," I had been wavering on the relevance of the information. I had seen clearly the Universal Gravity Code and its disparaging effects on the human condition, but I thought I had been abandoned when I could not figure out how to disarm the Code or diminish its effects. My ego wanted a "ZAP" kind of a solution; my simple mind thought I would be given a magic pill, spell, device, or technique. So each day, in every way I could imagine, I repeated that question: *How do I disarm the Gravity Code?*

Now, as I looked at the words written on my journal page, it seemed that I had been given a direct answer from "The All That Is," or God. A shockwave went through me, for I understood that during my exploration I had been shown that hidden within mathematical physics equations and nature's governing laws are simple solutions to disentangle the despairing impact of gravity on the human condition, ultimately disarming the emotional encoding from our life's traumas.

The Understanding

I have come to understand that something deep inside me wants to be released. Maybe it is a distant memory, a long-forgotten story, or a conclusion to a story. If so, where did this story begin, and where will it end? Is it about an individual, or about humanity as a whole? This book is my exploration of these obscure thoughts and questions. I am in full knowledge that there are never definitive answers, only temporary new perspectives. May this little "ditty of life" be just that: a temporary separation from the phenomena we call gravity.

There are four sections to this book. The first is that whimsical account of Isaac Newton's life, a time in history that may have come from my overactive imagination, or perhaps from the buried truths of our Universe. The second section describes the human condition as it pertains to these truths. The underlying meaning has been said before in many different manners by many different teachers. The last two sections of this book came to me after much inner and outer deliberation. I had slipped into a personal identity crisis, and I could not understand how I would have been shown the first part of the book but not be given a remedy or way out. This is when I stood powerfully on the mountaintop and, as mentioned, asked the Multiverse a thousand times in a thousand different manners, "HOW DO WE DISARM THE GRAVITY CODE!?" Oh, so slowly, I fell into the understanding that I had been given the magic key in a progression of synchronicities, teachings, relationships, and finally, the divine message. Most importantly, Isaac's laws had given me a roadmap.

The Term "Know"

As you read the pages that follow you will see that I have purposefully capitalized the words "Know" and "Knowing" in some sentences. The word "know" is knowledge of the mind, information that we have obtained through study or life experiences. When I use the capitalized word "Know," I am referring to wisdom bestowed on me which may not make logical sense but whose meaning has had a deep spiritual impact on me. I believe the source of this "Knowledge" is of another dimension or the benevolent energy I refer to as God.

The Many Names of God

I have purposefully used a multitude of words to describe the essence or energy known as God. Each of the names has an attribute of what my awareness Knows as God. Other references include I Am, Presence, Creator, Spirit, Multiverse and All-Knowing.

Possibility** Knowing** Releasing** Freedom

This is the pattern of life and of this book. We begin our journey with the exploration of the possibility of the existence of the Universal Gravity Code. We then move into the Knowing of the manifestation of this gravitational code. Then we can release the bondage to the illusion, and finally, dance in the freedom of weightlessness.

> *"I don't know what I may seem to the world, but, as to myself, I seem to have been only like a boy playing on the seashore, and diverting myself in now and then finding a smoother pebble or a prettier shell than ordinary, whilst the great ocean of truth lay undiscovered before me."*
>
> *- Sir Isaac Newton*

PART I

Explore the Possibility

"Truth is ever to be found in simplicity and not in the multiplicity and confusion of things."

-Sir Isaac Newton

I | EXPLORE THE POSSIBILITY

CHAPTER ONE

━━━━━⊰❧⊱━━━━━

What If

Isaac Newton's most famous experiment, the *experimentum crucis*, demonstrated his theory of the composition of light. While in a dark room Newton briefly allowed a narrow beam of sunlight to pass from a small hole in a window shutter through a prism, thus breaking the white light into an oblong spectrum on a board. Then, through a small aperture in the board, Newton selected a given color (for example, red) to pass through yet another aperture to a second prism, through which it was refracted onto a second board. What began as ordinary white light was thus dispersed through two prisms.

Newton's "crucial experiment" demonstrated that a selected color leaving the first prism could not be separated further by the second prism. The selected beam remained the same color, and its angle of refraction was constant throughout. According to Dr. Robert A. Hatch of the University of Florida, Newton concluded that white light is a "'Heterogeneous mixture of differently refrangible Rays' and that colors of the spectrum cannot themselves be individually modified, but are 'Original and connate properties.'" [1]

---

[1] Retrieved from http://users.clas.ufl.edu/ufhatch/pages/01-courses/current-courses/08sr-newton.htm

Behold an entry from the secret diary of Sir Isaac Newton, plucked from my imaginings:

It's late August, the year of our Lord, 1666. I find myself tormented by grave times; the gravity of the state of our world is suffocating, to say the least. The scourge of the plague continues to run rampant. Once again, Cambridge has closed its noble doors in hopes of curtailing the spread of the dreaded disease. I have been forced to find repose at my family's farm in Woolsthorpe, Lincolnshire. Outwardly I show my disgust at the thought of losing precious time in my research due to the closing, though secretly I must admit that I find this time to be a reprieve from the mundane mathematical theories of my professors and colleagues. This stay has afforded me the chance to devote the majority of my time to my alchemy studies.

I have spent most of my days pensively meandering through my mother's gardens reflecting on the potential global impact of my recent findings. I have kept detailed accounts regarding my extraordinary enlightenment, but I have deep trepidation about sharing this work with anyone. I am especially reluctant to share these conjectures with my colleagues, for fear of being shipped off to London and committed to Bethlem Asylum. I have to question myself, has madness set in? Were the visits with the beings made of light delusional? No! I know that I am on the verge of something spectacular, as if I am standing at the precipice of a new world order with universal impact. I sense the utterings of EUREKA gathering in my belly ready to be bellowed out for the entire world to hear.

I must still my nerves and control my angst. I must compose my thoughts and determine how I will present these findings to the world. I have been hit in the head by the fruit of the tree of knowledge. It is impossible to "un-know" a truth which has been bestowed on a soul level.

1 | WHAT IF

This had truly been an *annus mirabilis* ("miraculous year") at Woolsthorpe Manor. While reposing in the shade of the apple trees on the property, Isaac recalled how this "insanity" all began with his "crucial experiment." Not in a million years would he have imagined that the procurement of the toy prisms at the open market would have led to the unfolding of his current understanding. The events which had followed still had him quaking in his boots. Isaac quietly reminisced about the day the light entered into his world.

He saw it all re-enacted in his mind, like a vision….

Hannah gasped as the library chamber door slammed shut in her face.

"If I've told you once, Mother," Isaac shouted, "I've told you a thousand times! Just leave me to my business!"

My God, My God! He may be insane! Hannah thought, her eyes welling with tears. She gave herself over to them, folding herself into an overstuffed chair just outside the library door and sobbing heavily into her hands until she was spent.

"All I wanted to do," she said as she lifted her gaze to the massive wooden door, "was to pull the draperies open, allow a little sunlight into the room. It is not right for him to be in there day after day in the darkness of those chambers. It is just not right."

Then, as she reflected on the history of his melancholy and mental imbalance, Hannah turned her questions on herself. "Was it a grave fault to have allowed Isaac to return to the sanctuary of Woolsthorpe Manor?" She paused for a deep soulful sigh. "Maybe I can lure him into the gardens this afternoon. He seems to find peace when strolling amongst the apple trees and the gardens. That is it; I will come back at teatime and ask him to go for a walk with me 'midst the trees."

As Hannah conspired about the means to get Isaac to leave the library, Isaac continued to set up for the day's experiment, all the while murmuring to himself as if he was speaking to another.

"I just know today is the day that I will see the light. It was clearly revealed to me in my dream last night. I just have to strategically place everything in their correct positions. The correct positioning will allow the sunlight to stream in through the tiny slit which I made in Mother's shutter and then to flow through the prism. I will watch for the spectrum of colors to expand and form on the white board. The trick will be to isolate one of the colors to pass through the additional slit I have made in the white board. Then, the isolated color will pass through the second prism and reflect its light on to the other white board across the room. I will be able to demonstrate without a doubt that the prism does not make or distort the colors. I will prove to the world that the white light from the ray of sunlight is indeed heterogeneous, a mixture of differently refrangible rays, and that the colors of the spectrum cannot be modified."

Everything was set. Excitedly, Isaac waited for just the right moment when the sun would be in position to cast her rays through the tiny hole in the shutter. Then it happened! The light streamed in, hit the prism and shone its beautiful rainbow of colors on the board. Isaac ran to the other side of the room to adjust the slit to isolate one color. He watched as the green ray of light from the well-positioned slit shone through and passed through the second prism. Eureka! The color on the second board remained green. No change had happened! Isaac let out an earth- shattering yell.

1 | WHAT IF

"I WAS RIGHT! I WAS RIGHT! DO YOU SEE WHAT I HAVE PROVEN! I WAS RIGHT!"

Hearing Isaac's shrieks, Hannah came running through the library door and in the process knocked over one of the boards, which bumped into the window shutter, allowing the light of day to brighten the dark and dusty chambers.

"Isaac! Isaac! What has happened?"

"MOTHER!" Isaac bellowed. "You have ruined everything! GET OUT! GET OUT! SHUT THAT DOOR AND NEVER COME BACK!"

In utter terror, Hannah ran out of the room, sobbing and yelling, "Dear God, he *is* insane! Oh, dear God!"

Isaac threw himself down onto the settee in the corner of the room and tried to calm the rage he felt pulsing through his veins. He was infuriated that his mother had ruined his moment of triumph. He laid there with his eyes tightly closed, trying to regain his composure. He couldn't be sure how much time had passed, but suddenly he sensed that there seemed to be a brilliant light illuminating the room. As his eyes flew open, he felt his fury rising once again. Isaac was fully expecting to see his mother, opening the heavy draperies. Instead, there before him was a brilliant white light which seemed to be coming from nowhere and everywhere at the same time.

Shielding his eyes, Isaac questioned, *What form of phenomena is this?* Squinting and barely able to focus on the light, he saw that within the brilliance of the light was the shape of a being.

Is it a man? How did he get in here? Isaac wondered, then, with a trembling voice, he asked, "Who are you?"

"I am Iahhel, the Angel of Knowledge, and the patron angel of the desire to know. I am a messenger from The All-Knowing. I have been sent to help you rediscover the universal knowledge that has been forgotten long ago. I am a guide to philosophers and those who are attracted to mysteries. I, Iahhel, can guide you to enlightenment."

Isaac repeated this question, though this time it was more a demand. "WHO ARE YOU?"

"I am a being of light," Iahhel replied, his voice soothing, "an angel of The All-Knowing, and you have summoned me. I was with you last night in your dream and you asked me to come to your aid today. You said it was crucial and that you needed The Almighty's guidance. Isaac, the All-Knowing has heard you and has a very important purpose for you. You will usher in a new era. We will bestow on you the lost knowledge of the Multiverse. We have been watching you, listening to you, and you have been chosen."

As Iahhel spoke those words, his light's essence refracted into seven rays of light, so that now standing before Isaac were seven additional light beings. Prompted by Iahhel, each light being spoke their name and the gift they bestow on the human race:

I am the 1st Red Ray, May the Power of God be with you.

I am the 2nd Orange Ray, May the Truth of God be with you.

I am the 3rd Yellow Ray, May the Love of God be with you.

I am the 4th Green Ray, May the Purity of God be with you.

1 | WHAT IF

I am the 5th Blue Ray, May the Wisdom of God be with you.

I am the 6th Indigo Ray, May the Freedom of God be with you.

I am the 7th Violet Ray, May the Peace of God be with you.

Iahhel then said, "Isaac, the purpose of your crucial experiment was to confirm your theory that sunlight contains light rays of differing colors and unequal irrefrangibility, which is indeed true here on Earth as it is in all the Multiverse. The crucial wisdom being bestowed on you today is that the pristine brilliance of The All-Knowing's white light consists of a rainbow of Rays that contains the frequency of each color and its attribute. These attributes are a reflection of our shared perfection with The Presence… 'As above so below.' The entire Multiverse has been called to remember their communion with the Almighty and to return to their innate essence with the guidance of these Rays."

That first encounter with the light beings had taken place seven months prior.

Now Isaac looked up at the apple trees and felt a peace within as he pondered the expansiveness of the information that had been imparted to him, and on the thousands of notes he had taken as he, Iahhel, and the Seven Rays had their daily meetings. He reflected on the fresh new lease on life he had enjoyed over the past several months, a glorious reprieve from his typical gloom and doom state. Isaac recalled that at Cambridge, he had made only one friend among his fellow students and that his notebooks were riddled with entries about his anxiety, sadness, fear, a low opinion of himself, and dark, sometimes suicidal thoughts. He now sensed that the influence of Iahhel's teachings and those of the Seven Rays had somehow lifted a heavy veil from his grave and miserable existence.

Isaac's thoughts then darted to the secret hiding place where he had stored the sacred diaries. As instructed by the light beings, he had carefully inscribed the symbol of Tau on each diary page and marked the hiding place with this same symbol. Isaac mentally retraced his steps and reassured himself that no one would stumble upon the diaries; they were safe until he was ready to share them with the world. In them, Iahhel had expounded the importance of the divine timing of the unfolding of the information. Not a moment too early and definitely not a moment too late. It had been written in the stars, Iahhel had said, and HE, Isaac Newton, had been chosen to usher in this new dawn for human existence on earth.

Isaac now had an understanding that we humans are just a facet in the All-Knowing's multidimensional Multiverse. The synchronizing of all planes depends on precision – not like that of a finally-tuned Swiss watch, but rather the precision and balance of nature. Isaac was proud to be such an integral part in the creation of his world, which he understood meant that he would be an integral part in the creation of planet Earth's future.

I | EXPLORE THE POSSIBILITY

CHAPTER TWO

―――◦❦◦―――

Gloom and Doom

As he lay under the shade of his favorite apple tree, Isaac recalled with some reluctance the official correspondence he had received from Cambridge earlier that week. Studies would soon resume, and Isaac found that the thought of returning and sharing his new findings with his professors and colleagues had begun to eat away at his enthusiasm. The thoughts and effects of the dark side of his personality were beginning to slither back into his awareness.

Isaac asked himself, *Can I do this? Will I have the inner strength to go against all of society? Who will ever believe that I have spoken to light beings? What if they don't believe me, or even ridicule me? They will likely call me insane.*

Slowly, like a snake in the grass, a shadow began to cover Isaac's heart. He fell into the all too familiar disempowering energy of self-doubt and self-loathing. Then the final thought came: *Who am I? I am not worthy to share such grandiose ideas and teachings. I am just the awkward imbecile I have always been…*

At that very moment, and certainly by no coincidence, young Isaac was hit on the temple by a falling apple, rendering him unconscious. The following is the conversation he had with the angel Iahhel during the time of his unconscious state.

"...And since Space is divisible in infinitum, and Matter is not necessarily in all places, it may be also allowed that God is able to create Particles of Matter of several Sizes and Figures, and in several Proportions to Space, and perhaps of different Densities and Forces, and thereby to vary the Laws of Nature, and make Worlds of several sorts in several Parts of the Universe. At least, I see nothing of Contradiction in all this."

"Yes, Isaac," Iahhel said, "You will write about this in a future published work, in 1704, to be called *Opticks*, but this is about the gravity, Isaac! Gravity!"

"I understand," Isaac replied. "I understand these are grave times, but I made clear notes regarding my thoughts and findings." He then recited from his notes: "'Why should that apple always descend perpendicularly to the ground?' Why should it not go sideways, or upwards, but constantly to the Earth's center? Assuredly, the reason is that the Earth draws it. There must be a drawing power in matter. And the sum of the drawing power in the matter of the Earth must be in the Earth's center, not in any side of the Earth. Therefore does this apple fall perpendicularly, or towards the center? If matter thus draws matter; it must be proportion of its quantity. Therefore the apple draws the Earth, as well as the Earth draws the apple.'"

"Isaac, did you not hear me? What about the other notes, the explicit notes I gave you regarding the GRAVITY CODE?"

"Yes. Yes, the moon, the stars, the Earth's core. All relative, I know, I know." Again he recited from his notes: "'Whilst I was pensively meandering in a garden it came into my thought that the power of gravity (which brought an apple from a tree to the ground) was not limited to a certain distance from Earth, but that this power must extend much further than was usually thought. Why not as high as the Moon, said I to myself, and if so, that must influence her motion and perhaps retain her orbit, whereupon I began calculating what would be the effect of that supposition.'"

"Isaac, you are not listening, and this is of the utmost importance. World order depends on the disarmament of the GRAVITY CODE! I entrusted you with the secret formulas to disarm it before it is too late. It is your life purpose to do so. Isaac, where have you hidden them?"

"I do not know of what you speak," Isaac answered. "My head hurts, and I hear my mother calling. I have to go now …"

"Isaac, we were depending on you. Remember 'Divine Timing' - the seal of Tau will not be opened again for another three-hundred-fifty-three years. Please, Isaac, you have to remember…"

Just then Isaac heard the faint sound of his mother's voice, calling to him as if from many miles away.

"Isaac! Wake up!" she exclaimed, shaking him by the shoulders. "Isaac! Are you alright, son?"

Isaac opened his eyes to see her concerned face hovering over his.

"Oh, thank goodness! You were out cold!" She placed a cool cloth on his forehead.

"Something hit me in the head…" he muttered groggily.

Hannah's eyes darted this way and that, then her gaze landed on an apple lying nearby. "Why, I suspect that apple fell and hit you in the head. Do you remember anything?"

"No, no, not really, just a silly dream about a theory I have been working on. I am fine, Mother, just fine."

But even as Isaac said the words, the details of the dream slipped further and further into the recesses of his mind. He lost all memory of the beings of light, the hidden diaries and his life purpose; they had all been covered with a thick veil of "not enough" and "unworthiness." Isaac forgot his Remembering and relented to the tide of the human condition. The extent of his delusional false self would now be the catalyst and birth of the age of the Newtonian Illusion.

In the background, The Universal Gravity Code churned away, undetected by humankind, slowly eating at the core of civilization as a worm eats at the core of an apple.

New World Math According to Ginger

The Law of Universal Emotional "Gravity" (as in these are "Grave Times")

This law states that an energy attracts every other energy in the Universe with a force that is directly proportional to the product of their emotional masses and inversely proportional to the square of the illusional distance between their heart centers.

The equation for universal emotional gravitation takes the following form:

$$F = G \frac{m_1 m_2}{r^2}$$

where *F(fear)* is the "emotional gravity" force acting between two objects, m_1 and m_2 are the masses of negative emotions of the objects, *r* is the illusional distance between their heart centers and *G* (God) is the constant.

> **Bottom line: you attract what you are. The stronger your negative emotional pull, the more Gravity you will experience.**

I | EXPLORE THE POSSIBILITY

CHAPTER THREE

The All Knowing Has Spoken

Upon Iahhel's return to the Crystalline Palace he was summoned to stand before the throne of the Presence Which Has No Name. There, Iahhel recounted his adventures with Isaac the human and the Seven Rays. He spoke of his perceived failure to disarm The Universal Gravity Code.

Iahhel threw himself down before the throne, run though with agony because he felt that he had failed and the Earth plane would be doomed and destroyed by the Gravity Code.

"The timing was perfect," he cried out in anguish, "The stars of the Milky Way were in perfect alignment, and the only thing left to do was remember."

Iahhel, knowing the ways of the Multiverse, struggled to understand how Divine Timing, Divine Intervention and Divine Purpose could not have bought all the pieces of such a perfect plan into place. Surely it was something he had done wrong, and he pleaded with the Presence to help him understand what that was.

Realizing that the earthly illusion had been placed over Iahhel's eyes, The Presence and the other light beings surrounded the angel in unconditional love and with a gentle embrace brought him back to his Knowing. In an instant, Iahhel realized he had never left the Crystalline Palace, he had merely been energetically interacting with Isaac in the zero-point gravity field. He remembered that time and space are but a subjective construct of the earthly collective unconsciousness and experienced differently depending upon the perspective of the viewer. And, finally, he remembered that his perfect purpose, along with Isaac's, was to BE right there in the eternal embrace of unconditional love, nothing more, and nothing less.

The Presence now addressed the heavenly consciousness that had gathered before the throne. "On the Earth plane, the constructs of time and space will begin expanding outward into the Multiverse until the veil of illusion becomes so thin it breaks apart. The emergence of the Rays and their frequencies of light, which are the attributes of unconditional love, will begin to permeate the earth plane. One by one the earthlings will begin to awaken to their true selves. No longer necessary, the Law of Gravity will be dismantled and humans will remember that there is no-thing holding them down from rising to new dimensional levels. Teleportation will be remembered, instant thought exchange will be remembered, and the constraints of time and space will be diminished. This will be the emergence of a new human race unencumbered by the illusion of separation.

"In the beginning there will be a few chosen individuals who will anchor in a new energy, a new frequency where love and light will penetrate even the darkest corners of the darkest soul. A choice has been made (remember there still exists free will) and the human race has chosen LOVE over FEAR. Iahhel's work with Isaac put this into motion. The law of critical mass will reverse itself and the disarmament of the Universal Gravity Code is eminent. The earth beings may need to get to the brink of destruction before they understand that the illusion of separation is a creation of their collective consciousness. As they approach critical mass, they will understand the impact of mob mentality and reverse its effects for the betterment of their species, once and for all dissolving the Earth plane's 'Self-Disassociation' and its consequences – grave times. The oppressive pressure of their 'Gravity' will wake them up and they will claim their divine connection and oneness with the Universal Being. Have faith, the salvation of the earthly world has already happened and need only be remembered."

New World Math According to Ginger

Ginger's definition of Critical Mass as it pertains to the Gravity Code

The relative magnitude of the mass (weight in the gravitational field) permeating our society's "grave" existence and the inhabitants of Earth has reached a dire point at which the chain reaction will self-sustain and perpetuate for eternity. If this mass is not reduced by recognizing it and debunking it, we will continue to spiral down… down… down. The gravitational pull will become such that humans will become oblivious to their divine nature and will lose touch with the heavens. No longer being subject to "gravity," the opposite shall also be true and the spiral will go up, up, up to true connection with unconditional love.

PART II

Embrace the Knowing

What is the Gravity Code?

"I can calculate the motion of heavenly bodies, but not the madness of people."

                                        -Sir Isaac Newton

II | EMBRACE THE KNOWING

CHAPTER FOUR

────❖────

Seeds of Dis-ease: The Germination of the Code

All mental, physical, and spiritual diseases are in one way or another related to trauma. How, where or when the seed was planted into our psyche or our physical or emotional body is irrelevant. To be clear, NO story – no matter how gruesome, destructive, horrific or seemingly soul-crushing – has any significance whatsoever. This may be a difficult concept to grasp, for why would the event or series of events that planted the seed/seeds of disease be without relevance? Wouldn't it be helpful, possibly even healing, to know the event, remember the event, and process the event? What I have come to Know is that the story's only purpose is to perpetuate the growth of the Universal Gravity Code. The Code germinates from the seed or trauma planted by the story, but never from the story itself; in fact, the story may even mask the actual code from being detected.

Hypothetical Scenario

The Story: "I am terrified of heights."

A ten-year-old girl disobeys her parents, climbs up on the roof of their house, falls off, and breaks her leg. The seemingly logical "moral" of the story is that when you disregard authority, bad shit happens.

The Gravity Code: "I am not enough."

The mental dis-ease created by the fall seems to be the fear of heights. I, however, beg to differ. The survivor of the fall is not fearful of heights because she fell off a roof as a child; she is afraid of heights because she has a gravity code of "I am not enough" being played out as "You are clumsy and not to be trusted with your own safety." The seed planted by the event was a lack of self-trust.

Retelling or processing the story over and over again will never get her back up on the roof. Reliving the pain of the broken leg she suffered and the residual pain that may plague her forty years later will not get her back up on the roof or, for that matter, cure her of the metal anguish manifesting itself as physical pain! The encoding of the seed shows up as mental and physical pain, and I am sure if we look deeper, the spiritual pain is right there too.

In fact, I can guarantee that this particular seed or code would have kept her from doing ANYTHING she perceived as potentially risky. As this could include any number of things, the fear of risk would possibly have a significant impact on her personal and professional life. The only thing that will get her back up on the roof is the decision or Knowing that she can trust herself and that she is safe in her own care. Once she is in that space, she would be healed of the encoding caused by the event, even if she never told the story again and even if she never addressed it with any mental health healing strategies, conventional or holistic.

How, you might ask, how could she be healed of something she doesn't face or deal with head-on? Nourishment, exercise, meditation, spirituality seeking, service to others, and joy through artistic expression are all means of disarming a gravity code. During these exercises the focus comes off the story, thus allowing the brain to begin creating new pathways that circumvent the code's programming. Then the life pattern created by the code becomes apparent and is no longer hidden. A threatened exposed code may and probably will try to fight back by creating a new similar pattern to replace the challenged old pattern. Consistency in our self-care practices will diminish the effects, compelling us to rise to higher levels of self-love. Self-trust is the result of self-love. By using such strategies as those mentioned above, you find the way back to balance. Not because you *resolve* your traumas, but because you *find* self-love and acceptance. The trauma dissipates, and you disengage from its effects as you become a more loving version of you.

The concept of unconditional love starts within and moves outward. Love comes from the eternal or Life Source Energy, moves into the internal (our inner being), and then out to the external world. This type of love does not have an opposite. What I speak of here is the unconditional love energy of our Creator.

The trick is to recognize the Gravity Code as it manifests in patterns, distortions, or "loops." Loops are the key, the hint, and the magic to transformation. Even if you have a trauma completely hidden deep within your psyche, it can be healed without ever realizing, remembering, or discovering the incident. Again, I am going way out on this limb and strongly stating that it never matters where the seed of trauma originated. Remembering, telling, or internally repeating the story only feeds the seed as it germinates, and unravels shoots and roots that can potentially affect all aspects of your wellbeing.

Here's another way to comprehend this theory of mine: Evel Knievel broke over four hundred thirty-three bones during his career as a stunt performer, jumping motorcycles from extreme heights and distances. With each new stunt he attempted to go higher and farther. This is a far cry from the little girl in the hypothetical scenario. You would think that after breaking the first hundred bones, a seed of fear of heights would have been implanted somewhere within him. This is what I am talking about – it is not the stories, the scenarios, or the bone-breaking that creates the fear. Fear comes from the accepted assumption or the emotional encoding. In the hypothetical scenario, the assumption being played out or looped is "I Am Not Enough." Evel Knievel had his seeds of fear germinating in their own unique way, but obviously his loops had nothing to do with a fear of heights.

Let's go on a little journey of self-discovery to recognize how the Universal Gravity Code and its endless patterns and loops may be directing your life and the lives of your loved ones.

II | EMBRACE THE KNOWING

CHAPTER FIVE

---ஜ்ஜ்---

The Endless Loop:
Recognizing the Universal Gravity Code

Though it can certainly appear that way when viewed from an earthly perspective, the Universal Gravity Code's encoding is not "evil." It is set in place to wake us up or, stated in today's terms, it is our "path to enlightenment." As a drunk or addict knows, rock bottom is the place where the illness has made them so sick, so tired, so destroyed that they seek a new way. They turn it over to their Higher Power, or surrender to love, and in doing so begin to reclaim control over their lives.

That is an interesting concept, and one that seems at odds with itself, for how can the act of taking control happen through surrendering? What the hell does surrendering mean anyway? Hadn't the woman in the earlier hypothetical scenario "surrendered" to her fear of heights?

The answer is no.

It is really important to get this crystal clear: the woman did not perceive a choice while she was victim to the fear of heights. She was in a gravity code loop, and her mind was telling her that she was justified for being afraid of heights, and perceived risks in general, because when she was ten, she got hurt while disobeying her parents. She hadn't surrendered or given into the fear; she perceived fear as *fact*. When you are stuck in a loop, you remain on repeat, replaying the same old scenario over and over again, both internally and externally. You are a prisoner to the Code. You are affected by something science calls *anosognosia*, which literally means "without knowledge."

Anosognosia is the most substantial barrier you face in overcoming the Gravity Code and its manifestation as a life loop or pattern. If you don't recognize that you have a gravity code, you really can't accurately see the need for a change. So now what?

Surrendering implies choice. The choice to surrender to "unconditional love of self" and to take even the smallest of action to participate in self-care begins the unraveling, decoding, disengaging, and the disruption of the Gravity Code. In the act of surrendering, you are blindly turning over your next best step and the outcome to the expression of love. I once heard someone say, "Faith is Freedom and Freedom is Faith." Again, this is an oxymoron – letting go of the reins gives you the control. We will dive deeper into this concept in the chapters to come, so look out, for you will be learning to unleash the power of the Multiverse.

Below is a shortlist of common loops. The actual list has no end, and it goes on forever. An essential notion in the idea of the Gravity Code's loops or distortion patterns is that they are found both in a single consciousness and the collective consciousness of a group. The mob mentality is a perfect example of a loop in the collective consciousness; others include racism, poverty, or fear of punishment.

5 | THE ENDLESS LOOP: RECOGNIZING THE UNIVERSAL GRAVITY CODE

Here are some common loops or codes found in individuals, family units, religions, work environments and/or society:

I Am Not Worthy	Too Hard
End of the World	Worst Case Scenario
Eminent Catastrophic Event	I Am Unprepared
I Am Unable to Clear My Mind	Fear of Loss
Body Image - Weight Too Fat Too Thin	No Motivation
I Am Tired - I Am Sleep Deprived	I Am Sick
I Am Not Enough – Not Worthy	I Am Damaged
I Am Not Whole – Vulnerable	Overwhelmed

The only way out, the only path to sanity, peace and pure love, is to get off the roller coaster. You cannot fix, unravel or change the past by concentrating on what is wrong, what went wrong, how it went wrong, and who caused the wrong. The GRAND ERASER of all is the remembrance of the purity and divinity of your being. This golden path is in the impermeable divine love we share with our Creator. We are Love. This single discovery changes everything in a blink of an eye.

Finally, I ask you to ponder the following questions. Write them down, place them in places where you will see them regularly (a mirror, work desk, refrigerator, car dashboard, et cetera), and ask them over and over again for the next several days. Then take a moment to write down what you have discovered:

- *Who would I be if I gave up my deep-seated, fearful thoughts?*
- *Who would I be if I lost my perceived control?*

_____
_____
_____
_____
_____
_____
_____
_____
_____
_____
_____
_____
_____
_____
_____
_____

II | EMBRACE THE KNOWING

CHAPTER SIX

The Loop de Dupe

As mentioned in the previous chapter, the Gravity Code and its distortion pattern are usually not apparent to us and are typically hidden from our awareness. The good news is that you do not need to fight your gravity code or loop(s); the mere act of becoming aware that you have loops is the beginning of their unraveling. Even more significant is that you do not have to search for the Gravity Code. You simply need to focus on self-care, *period*! Could it be that simple? Yes, for as you turn your attention away from the seed (trauma or story), the underlying purpose of your code will begin to show its face. Yes, the loop always has a purpose, and a disparaging one at that.

When unchecked, the code becomes your *modus operandi*. It becomes your safe place, your protection from the so-called evils of the world. However, the protection is an illusion, and it will lead you to take the wrong actions, all the while unaware that these actions are merely proving gravity's case. You want to be right, and you want to be vindicated, so you will unknowingly create more gravity until what you have is a multilayered self-fulfilling prophecy. When you become more aware of the loop and its possible purpose, it will become increasingly harder and harder for it to sustain the subliminal structure. Yes, at times the loop or pattern may burrow deeper in order to escape detection, but if you continue to focus on self-care the purpose, and ultimately the loop itself, will dissipate.

Here are a few possible destructive purposes of the Code. I left some space at the bottom for you to write down your own as they come to light. What are we choosing to prove? Whatever the backstory is, the question to ask will be, "What am I getting from this?"

If I am sick, I don't have to show up.

If I am sick, I can't be magnificent.

If I am afraid, I don't have to try.

If I am stuck, I don't have to move forward.

If I am damaged, it's something evil's fault.

If I am damaged, I am unable to participate in a healthy manner.

If I remain overwhelmed, I am safe from doing more.

If I am sick, I will receive love.

If I am sick, I have an excuse.

If I am stuck, it is your fault.

If I am damaged, it's your fault.

If I am damaged, I have a purpose or plight.

If I am overwhelmed, I can't show my genius.

If I am afraid, I can depend on others to save me.

_____

_____

_____

_____

The bottom line is that your loop or gravity code is always about fear, coupled with the presumption that "I am not enough"; "I will not be loved"; or "I am not smart or strong enough." The Gravity Code is a distortion of the truth, as in "My husband will leave me if I'm whole and happy," or some other warped version of reality. Then, just when you think you have discovered your loop and are ready to move on, it shows up in a new, usually more intense way and with even more proof of its existence. As you work through the next chapters, be very careful that your sneaky code isn't looking for a new inroad into your mind, for example, "All is well at home, so let's create worry over a catastrophic world event."

Worry/Fear/Anxiety about *anything* is a distraction from your true essence, which is one of Love and divine peace. These words are not just for you; they are for me and all who will listen. The idea that you are alone in this is just another illusion of the Gravity Code. We all are potential victims. Acknowledging the presence of the gravity code is the gateway to exiting its control and entering in the beautiful space of surrender.

Case: The Shit Show – It's Too Hard

This character has a million reasons why their particular problem exists, who is responsible for it, and what could be done about it if it wasn't so hard. They live in the space of "eternal" internal chaos and overwhelm.

When the "It's too hard" loop goes undetected, it will spiral out of control to prove that IT IS IMPOSSIBLE to solve or dissolve the problem.

Below is an example of such a loop. The woman in this case in point is worried about finances since losing her high-paying job, and because she feels her husband's career choice is an unstable one. As is often the case, this loop extends to other, related areas of life, including the cost of her house, which she loves, and the activities of her neighbors, whom she hates. Read the following statements out loud (noting the overpowering run-on sentences), and fast (as if frantically overwhelmed).

- I want a high paying job again, but I was burned last time so I'm not sure if I want to work or can be trusted with my choices. I now find myself in a low-paying position that takes up all my time so I never have a minute to focus on my financial situation or look for other employment. (Proof that "It's Too Hard")

- We overpaid for our house, so I don't know if we can get out of it or make money on a sale. What if my credit is too bad and I can't get a loan for another house? What if it won't sell for what we paid for it and the market might get better, but then I heard it might get worse, and I'm afraid it won't pass an inspection because there is work to be done in the attic and I don't want to move on this until I have looked at every angle and talked about it for two years. (Proof that It's Too Hard)

- The neighbors are horrible, drug dealing behind the house and always throwing noisy parties. I installed cameras so I can watch their comings and goings and I joined a neighborhood watch and attended all the meetings so I can report them but I am still powerless. (Proof that It's Too Hard)

- Ah OH, I feel an awakening. I am beginning to understand my magnificence and potential through my new quest for spirituality and authentic living. Over the past several months, I have found self-care and self-love by attending support groups, workshops and spiritual gatherings and my newfound wisdom is painting a rosier picture. During an energy healing session, I heard the wisdom of my ancestors proclaim that the road to joy is through an Open, Honest and True relationship with self and others. But how is this ever going to work out? My husband just got canned, we have one month to sell a house, find a new job, and a new place to live. We're moving towards bankruptcy and homelessness, or living in whatever dive we can afford on my flimsy salary. And I haven't been feeling well lately, I always have a stomachache or a headache or some ache somewhere. (Proof that "It's Too Hard" just got harder.)

Where is rock bottom, what will be the wakeup call? For each of us it will be different, just as the reason we ended up here is different, but the golden path out is and will always be the same.

The Shit Show is an actual scenario, and the story got WAY worse before it got better. The intensity of the effects of the Gravity Code became so powerful that a marriage ended, a beloved house was lost, physical and mental health suffered, and there was an extreme loss of income. The Shit Show is also a story of perseverance and complete surrender. Rock bottom hit hard but opened the most remarkable space for expansion and unconditional self-love. Many of the guided messages contained in this book came through as I bore witness and supported the heroine of this story, bestowing the glorious gift of knowing and observing the power of transformation held within the divine gift of this grave time. It was not an easy path – some may call it a "dark night of the soul" or a "surrendering to the angel of death" – but a definite ongoing victory over her "Shit Show" is transpiring, *poco a poco*.

II | EMBRACE THE KNOWING

CHAPTER SEVEN

Four Characteristics of a Gravity Code

All gravity codes have four similar components in varying degrees. The degree or level of severity is dependent upon the trauma, depth of the initial seed, or the need for the purpose to remain in place. As you uncover your gravity codes or their destructive purposes, try and decipher where they fall in each of these categories. Doing so will give you in-depth information on how your loops are functioning in your life. The more you illuminate the effects the Code has on you and your relationship with life, the better equipped you will be to circumvent its destructive purpose. These components are:

Fear · Disconnect · Perception · Co-Dependency

Fear

In the spectrum of all emotions, FEAR is at one end and LOVE is at the other. These two emotions cannot hold the same space. Yes, you can bounce back and forth at a rapid pace, but just as you cannot sense pain in two areas in your body at the same time, you cannot feel fear while experiencing true love.

What I have been shown is that there are three levels of fear (there are probably subsets to these levels as well, but we will keep it simple). As you take a closer look at discovered loops, distortions, or gravity codes, try to decipher under which level they fall.

3 Levels of Fear

Superficial	Engrained	Deep-Seated
Surface	Experiences/Religion	Undetected
Startled Reflex	Flight or Fight	Irrational beliefs
Intuition	Instinct	Faulty Wiring
"Boo! I Scared You!"	"I'm Out of Here!"	Hide-n-Seek

We often misuse the word fear to describe other emotions. It is essential to decipher whether what we are feeling about a given situation is actual fear or something else, the reason being you cannot reason with fear; it will not let go of its grip until the underlying purpose of the Gravity Code has been disarmed.

Here is a test I devised to determine if your perceived fear is genuine. I use it with my grandchildren all the time.

Place one hand on your tummy and one hand on your heart area. This hand positioning will direct your attention to the energetic impulses happening in these areas. Ask it a few questions. "Am I really afraid to _____?"; "Does the thought of _____ make me scared?"; et cetera. Feel, sense, and observe, take note of the sensations. Then ask, "Or, am I excited about _____?"; "Do I feel anticipation about _____?"; et cetera. Now, observe and feel the sensation you are feeling about an event or situation.

In my experience, excitement or anticipation have the physical sensations of tickly or fluttery feelings in your tummy, as in the saying "butterflies in your tummy." When you sit with this feeling for a moment, you may notice that your heart is racing a little but it is not an uncomfortable feeling. Observing excitement or anticipation usually ends with you smiling as you examine the questions and your physical responses. On the other hand, true fear intensifies its grip as you observe it. The sensation in your tummy may be one of rolling and constriction. Your heart is pounding and you feel tightness in your chest. The body has an intense visceral response to fear.

Observing and understanding your physical reaction to emotions is a means to unravel your encoding and their loops.

Notes:

_____

_____

_____

_____

_____

_____

_____

_____

_____

_____

Depth of Disconnect from the Remembrance of Your Divinity

As you progress through life, you are continually being fed many deceptions. Parents, teachers, spiritual leaders, religious groups, political groups, employers all unknowingly may have participated or continue to participate in diverting your Knowing away from your true essence, one of divinity. You were created in the likeness of God and composed of all the same miraculous components. Disconnection from the truth of who you are on any level impairs your ability to understand your divinity and the power that has been vested in you. The degree to which this disconnect or these distortion loops have impacted your psyche falls somewhere in these three levels.

3 Levels of Disconnect

Self-Esteem (Narcissism - God's View)	Contact Manipulation	Narcissism (World's view)
Deep Connection to Oneness and Self-Love *(See the explanation of narcissism in Part III – Chapter X)*	Rules and Regulations to Obtain Divinity	Excessive Criticism (You are Evil/Not Worthy)

Notes:

_____

_____

_____

7 | FOUR CHARACTERISTICS OF A GRAVITY CODE

World Perception

You possess the ability to alter your perception of anything and everything, and this is where free will comes into play. Your life lessons may have distorted your perceptions, or your perceptions may have been imposed on you by others, but ultimately, we choose. Embracing this understanding is the way to reconnect with your divine self. In what way is your gravity code veiling your world?

Benevolent	Both	Malevolent
Half-full	Teetering between both worlds	Doom and Gloom
Rose-colored glasses	Dichotomy	"Get the Bastards!"
Good	Good and Evil	Evil

A Guided Meditation
The Vision

Close your eyes, take in a few deep, deep belly breaths, releasing and letting go. That's it… allowing yourself to gently slip into a very relaxed state. Relaxing, releasing, and letting go. Deeper and deeper into relaxation. You are comfortable and feel safe.

For a moment let us imagine or pretend that we can see, feel and experience the gravity of your unhealed self. You are safe; this is only your imagination.

See yourself standing, facing a dark, dingy wall with a solid closed door; it looks/feels like you are in a cave or dungeon of some sort. The room is dark, dank, and the air has the heavy stench of gloom. You are crying, pleading, and waling to be set free. The words, emotions, and cries for help are coming from deep within your being. The sense of hopelessness is overwhelming. Part of the despair is the idea that your pleas have not been heard or may never be heard from this deep, dark place/space. You are pleading and yell out "God HELP me", but you do not understand how that could even be possible. You speculate that this may be your destiny or eternity. The depths of your despair are oppressive and soul-crushing. The weight and gravity of the entire Universe are pressing down on you.

Now, you hear/sense, someone, from behind you say ... "Turn around." You tremble with the fear of what you will see. At least the wall isn't a scary monster or demon of some sort. So you ignore what you heard and start screaming louder, with more intensity. But the quiet voice continues to gently say, "Turn around." You try to drown out the soft voice and scream, "DEAR GOD HELP ME!" but once again you hear, "Turn around." The sound of the gentle voice is compelling, and something inside you wants to listen.

Oh so slowly, you begin to turn around with your hands covering your eyes. With extreme trepidation, you slowly open your hands, then your eyes. Instantly you are immersed in the most powerful, illuminating light. As your eyes begin to focus, you see/understand that there is no wall on the other side of the room or this space, just an open expansion of brilliant white light. The light seems to be coming from everywhere and to everywhere. You also begin to feel physically light, as if you could fly. The feeling is exhilarating yet scary. You question yourself, how did I not see this before? I must be hallucinating.

Doubting what you are experiencing, you turn away from the light. The familiarity of the solidness of the wall, the air, and the floor are momentarily comforting, and you feel safe; then once again, you are overtaken by the feeling of gloom.

And you hear ... **"Turn Around."**

An audio version of this and other guided meditations can be found on my website: vadamsenterprises.com.

7 | FOUR CHARACTERISTICS OF A GRAVITY CODE

Earlier in my life, when I was submersed in the murky waters of gloom and doom, blame throwing and condemnation of my delusional dungeon, I was contributing to and amplifying all that I saw wrong in the world. In doing so, I was adding to your pain and the pain of the world. Today I have a deep understanding that I am part of God's creative force. The output of my energy constructs my reality, and your reality, and the reality of the collective consciousness is affected or constructed by the output of my energy as well. Each of us is a unique panel in the quilting of the Multiverse, yet we are part of the whole.

As I choose to see only Love, be only Love, walk, and talk Love, I change my vibration, and I experience the vastness of unconditional love of the Multiverse. As I experience this new love vibration, the gravity of this plane lifts, immersing me into profound gratitude, and I will receive. Genuine gratitude becomes the conductor of the energetic incoming flow of abundance, Love, and all that is whole, perfect, and good. It is my "comfort" vibration, my prayer. There is no need to proclaim what I want/need/wish to change or receive. I just become the vibrational match to the loving embrace of our Creative Force (what I call God) and my reality (my perception), and what I will receive will flow in with grace. My inward flow now matches my output. I am ready to inspire you. (*Psssst ... Turn around. No really, turn around.*)

Notes:

_____

_____

_____

_____

THE UNIVERSAL GRAVITY CODE

Level of Co-Dependency

In all relationships, we play a part in the Co-Dependency sliding scale, the ultimate goal being to stay as close as possible to the middle. In a balanced state, we can partake in a relationship without losing any aspect of self. There is no bending or warping of self to satisfy the needs of the other, and there is no demand for another to change for us.

When a relationship is out of balance, however, one person's wants and needs are squashed as the other takes advantage. This is what is typically described as a co-dependent relationship, and it can occur between friends, life partners, lovers, and family members. Codependency can also be an aspect of a relationship with large groups or entities, such as religions, political movements, et cetera. A relationship that slides out of balance can often include emotional or physical abuse, with each person participating on one side of the scale or the other as victim or the abuser. All gravity codes place us out of balance on this scale. Which side of the scale does your predominant distortion place you?

Sliding Scale

Codependent ———— Balance ———— Abuser

Codependent	Balanced	Abuser
Worthless unless needed	Both find value	Needs met by others

What have you discovered about your life patterns, or gravity codes? Were you able to uncover and understand their possible purpose as you looked at them through the lens of Fear, Disconnect, Perception, and Co-dependency? Take a moment to write down your discoveries.

_____

_____

_____

_____

_____

_____

_____

_____

_____

_____

_____

_____

_____

_____

_____

_____

_____

_____

PART III

Release the Illusion

Disarming the Gravity Code

Rose-Colored Glasses

"This is what we call love. When you are loved, you can do anything in creation. When you are loved, there's no need at all to understand what's happening, because everything happens within you."

– Paulo Coelho, The Alchemist

III | RELEASE THE ILLUSION

CHAPTER EIGHT

It's Time to Wake up… NOW!

"Self-Love work is to reach a space of knowing that "I AM ENOUGH"; I am enough in ALL ways, just as I am, I don't need to impress anyone. I don't need to get people to like me. I LOVE and ACCEPT MYSELF JUST AS I AM."

- Dr. David Hamilton

Guided Meditation
The Spiral

Here is another way for us to look at how The Universal Gravity Code holds us down. Close your eyes for a minute and visualize a spiral. The top of the spiral is like a funnel – open, with lots of information coming in. Now, as you saw in the Shit Show hypothetical, focus on one negative encoding or gravity loop with your full attention. With your attention fully on that grave thought or encoding, you will begin to spiral going down, down, down, intensifying the effects of the encoding. The spiral is like a cone, and it starts to funnel the incoming influences and information. The only thing getting through, the only thing down at the bottom, are the negative thoughts. As you spiral down, down, down to the bottom, you will find that your code of I am not worthy, I am not *enough, or fear of the unknown has planted and pinned you to the earth, like an elephant sitting on top of your chest, making it so that you can hardly breathe. In this state you will see nothing else, you will feel nothing else, you will know nothing else except for the Code and its oppressive gravity.*

Now let's imagine how you can undo this, how you can go back up the spiral to the top where there is access to all information and all Knowing, where the comforting and loving thoughts reside.

With effort, you take in a breath and decide to let in just a little bit of the thought that I AM LOVE. The pressure seems to ease up just a little bit, making space for another breath and the thought that says I AM LOVE. Expanding just a little further, you can breathe in just a little bit more of the thought I AM LOVE. Ahhh… Expanding out further, you're feeling lighter, the weight on your chest is releasing. Again, you think the thought; maybe you even say the words out loud: "I AM LOVE." You take some time, and with every breathe you expand the thought, I AM LOVE.

The thought starts to balloon out; you can even visualize the balloon filling up full of LOVE. You keep blowing into it; you keep blowing into that balloon of love and it continues to EXPAND! You actually can feel it tightening, but it is the opposite of what you felt before, because instead of a pressure this tightening is expansive, just as a balloon grows tight as it stretches and stretches and stretches. And as you stretch with I AM LOVE, ah, oh, it almost feels uncomfortable. It almost feels as if you are going to burst. You ask, What will happen if it burst? What will happen to me? Yet you keep expanding, you keep releasing the fear. Now you take the biggest deepest breath in, knowing with every cell in your body that I AM LOVE. Expanding … Expanding that love … until, ahhhh, finally it bursts, and your love joins all the particles of the Multi-verse. You release and let go, and you understand that you are a sparkly part of our loving Multiverse. You are the Unconditional Love. Expand in that Knowing ... And so it is.

> *I suggest that you record your voice reading the above meditation and use it on a regular basis, or an audio version of this and other guided meditations can be found on my website: vadamsenterprises.com.*

"If only for a nanosecond, you could see yourself as we see you, all self-doubt would be washed away."

I found myself saying the above statement to a lady – a profoundly gorgeous human being both inside and out – after she'd listed all the ways in which she saw herself as broken. As I listened to her my mind instantly thought, *That little SOB Gravity Code! How dare it mess with this beautiful being?* Up until that moment, the only thing that I had witnessed from this lovely soul was the purest of unconditional love, acted out in the most magical way. Now that slimy, no-good Gravity Code was trying to tell me that what I was seeing, feeling, hearing, and experiencing was some type of figment of my imagination. It was saying that she was less, much less than the magnificence and perfection I had observed. I honestly could have slammed her shadow-self (not physically, of course, but the ugly invisible energy) down to the ground and pounded on it until it stopped spreading such vicious lies. (Wow, glad I got that off my chest! Not much love and light in this paragraph, I know, but I needed to express how defeated I felt watching something that my Knowing saw as pure Divinity being slandered in such a manner.)

Why, oh why can we not see our perfection, claim and embrace our magnificence and divinity? Just forty-eight hours before my encounter with that lovely soul's shadowy self, I was asking my daughter Christina this very question as we headed off for a much-needed weekend together at a secluded B & B.

As we were winding our way through the maze of cornfields on a country road, I said to her, "Why does it seem somehow wrong for me to boldly say to a group of people 'I AM A DIVINE CREATOR,' and that 'MY LIFE AND ALL OF ITS CREATIONS ARE DIVINELY INSPIRED. I AM DIVINITY!'"?

My daughter gasped and said, "You can't say that!" Then, after she thought about it for a moment, she recanted and agreed. The writing of those statements on paper feels awkward; all of my false programmings tells me that those are "egoic" statements, bordering on "narcissism." Now I have to ask, *What is narcissism? Can there possibly be two twists to one word, as I have found in the word gravity?*

What I have to come to Know is that false programming creates an illusionary world that dictates every aspect of our lives. It is a world where the codes of "I am not enough" and "Never can be enough" are running in the background, basically undetected; a world where the truth is obfuscated by illnesses, traumas, and socialization. That truth is that each of us is "One of Divinity" and "One in Divinity," a divine spark experiencing life on this earthly plane, playing out a few chosen roles in the pursuit of remembering our true nature. To do so, we must pierce that illusion, that veil, that often seems impenetrable.

The only way I know to arrive at a personal space that releases such deep-seated feelings of doubt is to begin a crusade of self-love and acceptance. To simply love who you are right now, with all the quirky differences and labels you have placed on yourself or you have allowed others to put on you. As you begin this crusade, you will slip into a space where you can surrender to the silence, peace, and nurturing of knowing that YOU ARE LOVE, and you will find your freedom.

The simplest way I can say this is it's time to find a pair of Rose-Colored Glasses and begin to see the world with the eyes of LOVE and Gratitude. The tricky trick, and the most profound act of acceptance you can perform, is to turn around and look at yourself in the mirror with those rosy glasses. It is time to fall in love with your Divine Self.

On our drive home from our weekend adventure at the B & B, Christina and I had planned to listen to Paulo's Coelho's *The Alchemist.* I had referenced a quote from the book the previous week in my blog, and I was excited to listen to it again to see what tidbits it had for me this go-round.

I didn't have to wait long, because the very first passage of the book hit me over the head.

The Alchemist picked up a book that someone in the caravan had brought. Leafing through the pages, he found a story about Narcissus. The alchemist knew the legend of Narcissus, a youth who knelt daily beside a lake to contemplate his own beauty. He was so fascinated by himself that, one morning, he fell into the lake and drowned. At the spot where he fell, a flower was born, which was called the narcissus. But this was not how the author of the book ended the story. He said that when Narcissus died, the goddesses of the forest appeared and found the lake, which had been fresh water, transformed into a lake of salty tears.

"'Why do you weep?" the goddesses asked.

"I weep for Narcissus," the lake replied.

"Ah, it is no surprise that you weep for Narcissus," they said, "for though we always pursued him in the forest, you alone could contemplate his beauty close at hand."

''But... was Narcissus beautiful?" the lake asked.

"Who better than you to know that?" the goddesses asked in wonder. "After all, it was by your banks that he knelt each day to contemplate himself!"

The lake was silent for some time. Finally, it said:

"I weep for Narcissus, but I never noticed that Narcissus was beautiful. I weep because, each time he knelt beside my banks, I could see, in the depths of his eyes, my own beauty reflected."[2]

That passage sparked such an in-depth conversation between me and Christina that we didn't even get to the rest of the book. My guess is that we'd heard exactly what Spirit had intended for us to hear.

If society, and our own shadow selves, had their way, we would never be able to see the beauty of our souls. The challenge is that the only way to have a drag down fistfight with your gravity code, and the gravity codes of others, is to see your innate beauty and embrace your divine nature. Like Narcissus, you have the power to go against your false programming, fall to your knees at the bank of another human being, glance into their ocean of love, see your re-

---

[2] Coelho, Paulo. *The Alchemist*. New York, New York. HarperOne; Anniversary edition (February 24, 2015)

flection and revel in awe of your perfection; to simply fall in love with your divine self. In turn, humanity will look into the depths of your eyes, see the beauty of that divine self, and allow the salty tears of transformation to wash away the self-doubt so it too can see its true nature. Thus, we create a circle of LOVE.

> *"God created a circle of light and love so vast that no one can stand outside of it."*
>
> *– Carlos Santana*

Narcissism, when viewed through the lens of the Rose-Colored Glasses (eyes of love), is the embodiment of the acceptance, knowing, and unconditional self-love God had intended us to have. It is the ability to see through the illusion of this earthly plane, overcome the density of our physical bodies drop the attachment to self-deprecating thoughts, words, and actions, and joyously break the bondage of the Gravity Code.

It's time to rise up together and declare:

"I AM A DIVINE CREATOR AND CREATION!"

"MY LIFE AND ALL OF ITS CREATIONS ARE DIVINELY INSPIRED!"

"I AM DIVINITY!"

Did you say it out loud? No? Well, then let's try this again. Stand up, open your arms wide and bellow this out for all the world to hear. Own these statements, Know these statements, and now become the energetic imprint of these statements.

Then, take a moment to look into a mirror or body of water. Look deep into the ocean of Love in your eyes. What do you see? What do you sense? Do you see what I see? You are Love and Loved!

Thoughts:

_____
_____
_____
_____
_____
_____
_____
_____
_____
_____
_____
_____
_____
_____
_____
_____
_____
_____
_____

III | RELEASE THE ILLUSION

CHAPTER NINE

Pi in the Sky

Possibly one of the most destabilizing or derailing aspects of self-discovery is the realization of the impact that gravity codes have had on your life. This realization may throw you into a protection mode. Seeing the damage is "Soul Opening," to say the least, as is seeing the potential for growth if you break free of the code.

Like the other concepts in this book, I speak of this from experience. As I became aware of my patterns and programming, I also became aware of the potential for my life, and ironically this is what became my new roadblock. The concern over any damage caused by my codes was secondary to that of the who and what I could create. When I write this now, I realize how ludicrous this sounds, but back then my potential was terrifying. My "not enough" loops were about fear of the power within. For me, it was effortless to wallow in the "woe is me" of self-discovery; the trick was to move beyond that old story and create my desired reality. I want you to remember this; when the muck feels more desirable than eating pie, you will not be able to move forward to the bliss that resides in the obtainable "Pi in the Sky."

A phenomenon of your gravity code is that you falsely perceive it as your strength. You may boldly defend your stance because it is what keeps you safe in this particular space. Then, when you ask yourself to imagine a future of bliss, released of all gravity, a place where no-thing or no-one holds us down, you gasp at the potential and revert to fear.

Simple Meditation

Close your eyes for a moment and simply allow the Love of God (your Higher Power) to wash over you. Nothing to do or say ... just BE.

When you step into the vortex, quantum field, void, or the space of Source Energy, with no agenda except to feel the deep loving stillness of your Creator, you become One with All. In this space of unconditional love, you encounter the collapse of time and space and the expansiveness of the Innerverse. As you experience this space, you may begin to understand that creation is an energetic vibration, guided by an emotional charge (encoding). In this creative space, you could place a worldly intention to receive a new car, a billion dollars, a perfect partner, or you could surrender to the Knowing that there is nothing to desire. When you let go of the need to control and relinquish to simply BE in the essence and power of God's unconditional love, you find that there is no need to want for anything. You find yourself in a state of awe and wonder, allowing Love to flow as Love will, knowing that All is Well.

> *An audio version of this and other guided meditations can be found on my website vadamsenterprises.com*

If there was nothing to hold you back, what might you create with unlimited potential?

New World Math According to Ginger

Ginger's Pi (π)

Pi is the ratio of a person's external influence to their love awareness. Pi is a constant number, meaning that for all circles of any size, Pi will be the same.

III | RELEASE THE ILLUSION

CHAPTER TEN

The You Are Not Enough Bluff

If you could look at emotions under a microscope, you would see that all negative emotions are comprised of fear and that all positive emotions are comprised of Love. If you were able to look with an electron microscope, you would see that all fear-based emotions have the DNA encoding of "you are not enough," and all love-based emotions have the DNA encoding of divinity. And, if you could see subatomic particles on a Planck unit[3] level, you would see, remember and understand that fear and all its constructs are illusionary. Within the wholeness of the Multiverse or the vacuum of nothingness is the "Zero Point Field" – a vast emptiness where perfect, unconditional love resides and from which the spark of creation ignites.

Within our being is the opening or portal to the vast no-thing-ness. Within that silence is the essence of eternal or Source Energy. Unconditional love comes from this Source Energy; it moves into the internal (our inner being) and then moves out to the external world. We are ALL aspects of the divine spark of our Source; however, we must claim ourselves

---

[3] https://en.wikipedia.org/wiki/Planck_units

as such. Will you choose to remember that you are LOVE, despite all the programing that would have you forget?

It is from this forgetting of your true nature that every problem originates; it is in the remembering that every problem evaporates. Recall this paragraph from the first section of the book:

All mental, physical, and spiritual diseases are in one way or another related to trauma. How, where or when the seed was planted into our psyche or our physical or emotional body is irrelevant. ***To be clear, NO story – no matter how gruesome, destructive, horrific or seemingly soul-crushing – has any significance whatsoever.***

You are not your story; you are the strength or the inner power behind your story. You are the orenda, the mystical force which empowers you to move through your stories, injuries, and traumas and obtain the spiritual lessons they contain. You are one with Source energy, or what I call God.

Have you ever had a roller-coaster week, riding the highs of personal and professional accomplishments and simultaneously discovering the lows of your continued destructive patterns, or remnants of past stories? It never ceases to amaze me that the high points in life always seem to go hand in hand with my battle with my gravity code loops.

Remember, a gravity code is a pattern, known or unknown, that keeps you planted (or "pinned") to the concept of "GRAVE TIMES." Just as the earth's gravitational pull keeps you pinned to the earth's surface, this loop or encoding is what will inhibit you from rising and flying to new levels of love and experiencing your coexistence with the vibration of unconditional love, or your Source. These loops are born from the seeds of the human condition, as well as from your individual stories, injuries, and traumas.

One of my gravity codes will show up in a million different ways to demonstrate to me why I am not worthy. Some are huge plummets, as with the first drop of a roller coaster, while others are subtle "whoop de doos," bump after bump. Part of my evolution has been to become acutely aware of when I slip into times of self-doubt or self-sabotage. This heightened awareness helps me to stay on track and to continue to move forward on my life purpose path, even when it feels uncomfortable.

As mentioned earlier, some find it easier to stay behind the veil and experience the effects of self-doubt or self-sabotage rather than acknowledge and explore their innate magnificence. When you stay in this space of denial and disallowance of the authentic self, you are in misalignment with Source energy, which always leads to dis-ease on all levels – physical, mental, emotional, and spiritual.

Guided Meditation
The Stage of Life

You find yourself in the wings of a vast stage. There seems to be a massive production about to start. People of all sorts are rushing past you, fixing, arranging and setting up. You hear the stage director yell out, "MINUTES TO CURTAIN!" The whole scene is completely chaotic, and you look around for a place to hide and get out of the way.

Something draws your attention to the massive curtain stretching from stage right to stage left and from floor to ceiling. It is dark and all-covering. You can tell from the bottom and side hems that it is made of Royal blue velvet, though all that is apparent on the backside is a huge black surface. The weight of that curtain must be over a thousand pounds. Its immensity is overwhelming.

Suddenly you realize that someone has scribbled all of your innermost fears all over that curtain. You didn't see them at first, but now they are illuminated and somehow glaring at you. Fear of illness, Fear of financial failure, Fear of loss, Fear of catastrophic world events, Fear of the end, Fear of the beginning, Fear of losing a loved one, Fear of being alone... and on and on and on. You are afraid someone else will notice the scribbled vandalism and think that you were the one responsible. Your need to move away and hide is growing.

Just then, the stage director yells out, "CURTAIN!" and someone grabs your forearm and rushes you to center stage.

Your heart stops. "No, No, No, No, No!" you cry out, "I am not in this production! I cannot go out on stage!"

Now your heart is beating a million miles an hour and your hands are cold and clammy. The room tilts, and you are sure you might faint.

 Nooooo, I am not going out there. I don't even know what this is about, what am I supposed to do?

You see a slight glimmer of light peeking through where the curtains come together; you can hear noises of anticipation from the other side. Then – poof! – the curtain opens with a swish and you are blinded by the brilliance of the white spotlights. The crowd of beings who had gathered to witness this moment erupt into cheers, laughter, and applause. You slowly regain your vision, and you see, feel, and sense all of the love in the room is directed at you. Stand there for a moment and soak it in ...

You've made it. You have stepped through the heavy veil of Fear and have joined the radiance of the Light—no looking back now! You are the brilliant star performer of your life, your story.

> *An audio version of this and other guided meditations can be found on my website: vadamsenterprises.com.*

Thoughts:

_____

_____

_____

_____

_____

_____

Recently, I stepped out of my oh so cozy comfort zone and participated in several Facebook live sessions promoting Gratitude. I typically work face-to-face, and I love one-on-one, so doing those Facebook lives was a considerable amplification and expansion for me. During that same week, I led three live Gratitude Circles, attended a Writers Workshop, facilitated many Reconnective Healing sessions, and met with a new Practice Mentoring client. Then, for the grand finale, I gave my final approval for another book I was involved with.

Whooooo Hooooo, I was riding up the big hill of expansion with my arms waving in the air. Then I saw it, felt it, and knew it on a cellular level. I had been overlooking a deep-seated gravity code playing out in the background of my life story. During that week, a few of my professional and personal relationships amplified that loop. I won't bore you with the details, but I will say that as a "Healer," friend and companion, I can, if I am not vigilant, easily slip into a co-dependent relationship. One of the reasons that Reconnective Healing resonates so profoundly with me is that as practitioners we remove ourselves from the story and outcome and simply play with and become the catalyst of the frequencies, allowing these frequencies to do what is intended for that person at that particular time. It frees all parties, the healer and the healed, from co-dependency. Intuitive Mentoring, Professional Coaching, and Practice Management Consulting are a whole other ballgame, requiring extreme professional and emotional maturity to stay out of the story. At times I find this to be a challenge, particularly when I have deep love for the practice or person. I thought I was pretty good at maintaining those boundaries, until that "whoop de doo" week when I became aware of a gravity code of self-sabotage and "staying small" playing out in my life.

Though this newfound awareness felt like a slap in the face, I am eternally grateful for the a-ha moment it inspired. I realized that the way to maintain integrity with others and myself is to be authentically me at all times. I must always express myself honestly and lovingly – no playing small or pacifying myself or others. I learned I need to walk away when there is a misalignment and dive deeper when I am called to do so. My interactions will expand some – others, it will not – but I will always rise to a higher level of love when I choose to live authentically. This goes for you too, so whatever you do in life, always be authentically YOU!

During that same week, while chatting with my dearest friend, Marianne, I was given a Knowing. What I said to her with regard to one of her loved ones was the following:

"It is significantly more detrimental to a human's well-being to express themselves inauthentically and to do what is socially acceptable than it is to speak the unwanted truth. When you appease others and force yourself to do things or say things you are not truly feeling, you are injuring yourself. When you stuff down what you honestly think or feel and do something out of guilt, shame, and obligation, you plant seeds of destruction within your cellular body."

"Playing nice does not lead to wholeness. On the outside, it seems you're making amends or forgiving out of support for the other person. But this approach hurts both parties. Yes, forgiveness is key; first, you forgive yourself, then, with eyes of love, you forgive the other. That's it, that is your work. Then, when you understand and allow yourself to limit your interactions with someone, no matter who that person is to you, you honor your authentic self, which places you in alignment with your higher self and with Source energy. This alignment is the path to all healing and all wholeness. As you heal yourself, you make room for others to do their work and find wholeness."

As always, time and space are just an illusion – what is right for you today at this moment may not be right for you tomorrow. Just stay in the present and do what your Knowing shows you is right for you, NOW.

Is there an area in your life or a relationship where you have not been 100% authentic? How do you think you would feel if you could show up every day and with everyone as

YOU, no masks, no pacifying, and no pretending? What holds you back?

III | RELEASE THE ILLUSION

CHAPTER ELEVEN

Your True Self vs. Your Critic

"It's funny, the ins and the outs. It's like being shown a new color, no words you have to go back and experience it to try to find a way to explain it to others. I know what it is, but how can I have you share in my knowing?"

— Dr. Eric Pearl, Solomon Speaks

- Who are we?
- Will what we do in this life matter in the next?
- What is my life purpose?
- Is there a heaven where we can reunite with our loved ones, or does each soul get reincarnated over and over?
- What is my life purpose/meaning/vocation?
- Is there eternal life?
- Why am I here on earth?
- Just as we have a body made up of cells, are we as humans, the cells of our Creator?
- What is the question I should ask?

The questions go on and on and on, especially since each can branch out into several related inquiries. The point is, there will always be a question, an unknown, or a quest for greater understanding; it is part of our human nature to try to make sense of a seemingly senseless world.

In my experience, when someone is asking a question, they are usually assuming that there is a right and wrong answer. Our culture uses statements that encourage us to see things in black and white and avoid the grey areas. Furthermore, embedded in the concept of duality are the assumptions that everything has an opposite and that something cannot exist without the opposing side or view. We even use the term "polar opposite" to describe something very unlike the other, just as a magnet has two poles.

When you consider the two sides of your awareness, illuminated and shadow, light and dark or conscious and unconscious, you tend to see and/or understand them to be opposites, as in "good" and "bad." However, I have found that this idea is not as black and white as it may seem; for example, our hidden side or shadow self is not our opposite or our enemy, but our teacher. The unconscious patterns (good or bad) constitute the programming that will ultimately bring you closer to the understanding of *non-duality*, where nothing stands in opposition and everything is connected.

Below is a little theory of mine which I have based on both the Law of Attraction and the repulsion of magnetic fields. According to Wikipedia: [4]

Magnets are drawn along the magnetic field gradient. If opposite poles of two separate magnets are facing each other,

---

[4] Force Between Magnets. In *Wikipedia*. Retrieved from the URL https://en.wikipedia.org/wiki/Force_between_magnets

each of the magnets are drawn into the stronger magnetic field near the pole of the other. If like poles are facing each other though, they are repulsed from the larger magnetic field.

New World Math According to Ginger

Ginger's Magnetic Field:

Humans are drawn along the magnetic field of gradient. If opposite Personality Characteristics (PC) (illuminated/shadow, light/dark, or conscious/unconscious) of two separate humans are facing (interacting with) each other, each is drawn into a stronger field near the PC of the other. If like (similar) PC are facing each other, though, they are repulsed from the larger field.

What this means to me is that we do not grow into the more expansive field of oneness without facing or interacting with our shadow self or the shadow selves of others. We create a unified field when both are embraced. i.e.: opposites attract, and two wrongs don't make a right. Just maybe, the only way to enlightenment is through the dark tunnel, which opens into the expansive light. (Where have we heard that concept before?)

I have a question for you: In a "tit-for-tat" conversation, where opposing sides debate, offer justification for perceived wrong action, plea for vindication, and possibly become frustrated and angry, who is your adversary?

It is only through the embracing of your shadow self that you will become whole. I have realized that most of my life's conflicts have been about me shadowboxing the lady in the mirror. As my understanding of self grows, I am thrown off balance by fewer and fewer things, yet admittedly there are still people, circumstances and subject matters that continue to have me ready to throw up my fists and duke it out. The comical part of all of this is that when I say, "Put 'em up, put 'em up," I am really speaking to my so-called "inner demons" or the unhealed aspects of self. These aspects are what I have been referring to as my gravity codes or ego distortions.

I think it is safe to say that when you are in conflict with anyone or anything, the safest place to look for a resolution is within. Your way out of the emotional charge is to do a personal inventory and to see, feel, and know what about the situation is causing your need to fight back. When you tend to your internal conflict, the conflicts in the outer world begin to shift or lose their perceived potency. The only answer or solution to anything on this plane, or in this time-space continuum, is Love, and it begins with the love of self.

Thoughts:

_____

_____

_____

_____

_____

_____

_____

_____

III | RELEASE THE ILLUSION

CHAPTER TWELVE

―⋆―

The Blame Game

There is nothing like sitting with extended family for a lengthy period to get my victim mentality juices running. It never seems to fail. As far back as I can remember, I have had these same internal feelings. I see/feel my little girl self, sitting on the living room floor coloring as I listened to the Thanksgiving Day banter of my family. As they gathered, the churning of the negative feelings of blame ran through my veins. Of course, at that time I didn't know what I was feeling, I just knew I felt uncomfortable, and it seemed to be "their" fault. The difference now is that I am no longer unconsciously participating; I am quite aware of the effects that blame has on my mind, body, and energy field.

During the birth of my third grandchild, I took notice of my shadow (self) as I sat interacting with extended family. These interactions prompted me to dive deep and take a look at how blame has affected me, my loved ones, and the collective consciousness.

Blame is one of the most dis-empowering attitudes you can hold. Like many of us, you may have bought into the idea that by throwing blame on another you are hurting them and protecting yourself, but this is simply not true. In fact, whenever you blame someone or something outside yourself, you give away your power and move into a victim mentality. An attitude of blame will never get you what you want, nor will it heal your emotional pain or empower you. Furthermore, long-term blame is very destructive and toxic to your peace of mind and your physical health and wellbeing.

So how do we step out of a victim mentality and into a place of peace and love?

"Forgiveness ends all suffering and loss."

–A Course in Miracles, Lesson 249

<u>A Prayer to Release Blame</u>

(Based on Release, Heal and Transform Meditation by Barbara Clark)

It is only through a heart of forgiveness that I can begin to dissolve, clear, and release all my conscious and unconscious thoughts and feelings of blame. It is through forgiveness that I begin to see all the ways that I am holding onto blame. Forgiveness of others and myself exposes, clears, and releases the deep-seated and rooted ways that I am holding onto blame. I will no longer be consumed with the need to blame when I embrace a heart of compassion and forgiveness. The embodiment of blame will be disintegrated and cleansed from my physical and energy bodies through the power of forgiveness. My hardened heart, emotions, and energetic calcifications will be cleared and released through my forgiveness. My consuming need to point my finger outwardly will be softened, and my ability to turn inward will be transformed through forgiveness. My inner and outer lives will no longer be directed by blame when I walk in forgiveness. I will clear all ways that my blame is toxic to my body, mind and spirit. Through forgiveness, the pain and disease that may dwell in my body, caused by blame, will be healed and released. Through forgiveness, I am able to stop wounding myself with my blaming attitude. When I forgive myself and others, I am able to let go of all the ways I am still holding onto this blame even though it helps no one. Forgiveness will lead me to no longer fear letting go of blame. Eyes of forgiveness and compassion will show me that my blame and blaming attitude has never been justified. I am safe; I know that my blame or lack of blame does not justify what "They" did; only forgiveness can wash away and change outcomes. My new companions, forgiveness and compassion, will remind me that my blame only hurts me and not who or what I blame. I am ready now to let go of the poison we call BLAME.

I clear, heal and release any and all blame and aspects of blame that I have been holding in mind, body, and energy field. I now feel the immense power of the letting go of blame. I now empower myself and my choices. I now choose to forgive myself. I now choose peace. I now choose to feel peaceful and calm. I know that I am safe. I allow myself to soften and relax. I am compassionate with myself. I give myself and the world the gift of forgiveness. I choose to free myself from all thoughts and feelings of blame and regret. I forgive myself and take back my power. Peace, Love and Forgiveness are the gifts I give myself and the world. I am free from the attitude of blame. I am comforted, relaxed, and reassured. I am serene and centered. I embrace the energy of forgiveness and compassion.

An audio version of this and other guided meditations can be found on my website: vadamsenterprises.com.

When you stand in your power, washed of all guilt and blame, you become aware that your pain and suffering are just an illusion. When it is all said and done, you will remember that you are whole, perfect, and complete. You are worthy of love, you are worthy of compassion, and you are worthy of forgiveness. The only thing to forgive is that, for a nano-second, you believed that you were somehow disconnected from your Creator. It is time to wake up now, to remember who you truly are, to remember that we are all ONE with our Creator and ONE with all. **I am Peace, I am Love, All is Well.**

Incidentally, any mode of protecting yourself from the so-called evils of the world is a part of the BLAME GAME. Look closely; if you think there is an outside influence that has the potential to damage, harm, or affect you, then you would need protection. When you understand that there is nothing "NO-THING" that can change who you *truly* are, then you release the illusion of your need to be protected. With time you will come to Know that you are "the Way, the Truth and the Life" – the magnificent cleansing power of pure white light with all of God's colorful attributes. Nothing can diminish or amplify this power. You are the instrument, the crystal, the spell, the device, the mantra, the sage. Close your eyes for a moment, and KNOW that "I Am That I AM."

"I feel the Love of God within me now."

– A Course in Miracles, Lesson 189

This is the world the Love of God reveals. It is so different from the world you see through darkened eyes of malice and of fear, that one belies the other. Only one can be perceived at all. The other one is wholly meaningless. A world in which forgiveness shines on everything, and peace offers its gentle light to everyone, is inconceivable to those who see a world of hatred rising from attack, poised to avenge, to murder and destroy.

PART IV

The Process

Dance of Freedom

The Components of Unconditional Love

> *If a projectile were deprived of the force of gravity, it would not be deflected toward the earth but would go off in a straight line into the heavens and do so with uniform motion, provided that the resistance of the air were removed.*
>
> *– Sir Isaac Newton*

Guided Meditation
Activation of the Colors

Close your eyes, take in a few deep, deep belly breaths, releasing and letting go. That's it... allowing yourself to gently slip into a very relaxed state. Relaxing, releasing, and letting go. Deeper and deeper into relaxation.

Imagine a beautiful crystalline ray of white light coming down from the heavens and entering your crown chakra, washing over your entire body, and illuminating every cell in your physical and energetic bodies. Bask in the warmth and brilliance of the white light of your Creator. Now imagine that this white light refracts into many rays, reflecting the colors of a rainbow.... Each Ray of color presenting itself to you with the frequency and Divine attribute it beholds. These attributes are a reflection of our shared perfection with The Divine Presence. Allow yourself to see, sense and resonate with each color.

The color red washes over you from top to bottom and bottom to top, and you experience the frequency and essence of the 1st Red Ray, May the Power of God be with you.

The color orange washes over you from top to bottom and bottom to top, and you experience the frequency and essence of the 2nd Orange Ray, May the Truth of God be with you.

The color yellow washes over you from top to bottom and bottom to top, and you experience the frequency and essence of the 3rd Yellow Ray, May the Love of God be with you.

The color green washes over you from top to bottom and bottom to top, and you experience the frequency and essence of the 4th Green Ray, May the Purity of God be with you.

The color blue washes over you from top to bottom and bottom to top, and you experience the frequency and essence of the 5th Blue Ray, May the Wisdom of God be with you.

The color indigo washes over you from top to bottom and bottom to top, and you experience the frequency and essence of the 6th Indigo Ray, May the Freedom of God be with you.

The color violet washes over you from top to bottom and bottom to top, and you experience the frequency and essence of the 7th Violet Ray, May the Peace of God be with you.

Now imagine these rays integrating and harmonizing with your energy, as you become one with the pristine brilliance of The All-Knowing's white light. With the guidance of these Rays you are reminded that you are an integral part of the communion with the Almighty. Your shared perfection with The Presence of God – "As above so below."

An audio version of this and other guided meditations can be found on my website: vadamsenterprises.com.

IV | THE PROCESS

CHAPTER THIRTEEN

The Power of God

I begin this section of the book with a mild warning. If you are anything like me, reading and then trying to comprehend scientific theory is painful. I was stunned when my muse began to show me how laws of physics were to be used in writing this section. I have struggled with how best to relay information to you without overwhelming you with the source of my knowledge. I ask for your patience and indulgence as I first introduce you to a theory or law and then show you what was given to me with regard to the Universal Gravity Code.

Thomas Young (1773 –1829) first coined the term "energy." At the time of Newton, the concept of "energy" existed. Leibniz called it "vis viva". Both, Leibniz and Newton understood the process of energy conversion; for example, the kinetic energy of motion gets transformed into heat by friction.

Vis viva *(from the Latin for "living force") is a historical term used for the first (known) description of what we now call kinetic energy in an early formulation of the principle of conservation of energy.*

Energy comes in many faces:

- *Kinetic*

- *Thermal*
- *Gravitational*
- *Electromagnetic*
- *Rest Energy*
- *Nuclear*
- *Chemical*

Conservation of Energy

The conservation of energy implies that the sum of all kinds of energy of a closed (i.e. not interacting with something else) system is always conserved (as long as the system exists). Any particular kind of energy does not have to be conserved. There are no exceptions to this law!!! Never ever!!! Nowhere!!!

There is a fact, or if you wish, a law, governing natural phenomena that are known to date. There is no known exception to this law; it is exact, so far as we know. The law is called conservation of energy; it states that there is a certain quantity, which we call energy that does not change in manifold changes which nature undergoes. That is a most abstract idea, because it is a mathematical principle; it says that there is a numerical quantity, which does not change when something happens. It is not a description of a mechanism, or anything concrete; it is just a strange fact that we can calculate some number, and when we finish watching nature go through her tricks and calculate the number again, it is the same.

—The Feynman Lectures on Physics[5] [6]

---

[5] Feynman, Lectures in Physics vol. 1, 1963, p. 4–1
[6] https://astro.uchicago.edu/~gnedin/ASTR-BH/PDF/lecture2.pdf

The energetic charge of the Gravity Code is conserved within our emotional, energetic, and physical body as long as the structure (system) exists. Nothing is needed, feeds, or replenishes the energy of any particular gravitational code – no exception. The conservation of the energy within the structural system of the Gravity Code will not be modified or altered even if the body, psyche, or soul undergoes various changes. Nothing in the outer world can alter it. The only change or variance we may experience is the reaction to incoming action. The original form or energetic structure of the code remains the same.

Binding Energy

Energy has a sign; it can be positive or negative. Negative energy is also called binding energy. If an object has binding energy, some other energy needs to be expended to disperse or destroy that object. While nuclear/atomic or chemical energy can be positive or negative, gravitational energy is always binding; gravity always pulls things together.

If an object gets more massive or smaller, then its binding energy gets more negative. That results in production of some other energy. Conversely, to take a part of a gravitating object away requires an expenditure of energy. For example, to send a spaceship off the Earth (an asteroid off the solar system, a star off a galaxy ...), the expended energy should be converted into the kinetic energy of motion. The speed that corresponds to that energy is called the escape velocity. [7]

---

[7] Feynman, Lectures in Physics vol. 1, 1963, p. 4–1
https://astro.uchicago.edu/~gnedin/ASTR-BH/PDF/lecture2.pdf

Now we are getting somewhere. As mentioned above, gravitational energy is always negative (or binding); furthermore, that negativity increases when the size of the object changes; a byproduct of that is the creation of some other kind of energy. In the context of the Gravity Code, that other energy is dis-ease, be it physical, emotional, or spiritual.

What I have come to Know is that by introducing a different, more powerful or intense energy source we are able to convert that negative energy into a kinetic energy that, with the right application, will transmute and transform the energetic structure. In other words, I had finally found the answer to my big question: WHAT WILL DISARM THE GRAVITY CODE?

Life Force Energy

I believe that Life Force Energy is a combination of all energy, which was the theory presented by Leibniz when he spoke of Vis Viva, or Living Force. However, whereas he was referring to kinetic energy, I believe the term Living Force is a description of the BioField. The concept of an energy force, or field of energy, that produces life was embraced by ancient civilizations, and many cultures who call it various names such as prana or qi. Modern scientists have confirmed the existence of an energy – which they call the BioField – surrounding living organisms, and from what I gather many of them are busy theorizing how it is formed, be it from electromagnetic fields, a quantum vacuum, or a zero-point field.

The way I understand it, Life Force Energy is the intelligent energy from God the Creator to Creation. It connects us to everything in existence, and without it, there is no existence. It is detectable, palpable, and malleable. Another way to look at it or refer to it is the Unified Field of Intelligence. It is our essence, and it is God's essence.

This thought process led me to the following questions:

- What if there is no earthly or human manner to disarm the Gravity Code?
- What if the Gravity Code or the gravitational pull is God drawing us to the remembrance of our true nature?
- What if gravity is an illusion?
- What if the only way to alter, dismantle, or dissipate its effects is to introduce the energy of God's essence?
- What if this essence could be used to destroy the Code because it absorbs the energy?
- What if gravity is God? The emergence of God using Its essence to remind us that we are of this same essence? That we are God?

Professor Erik Verlinde, an expert in string theory from the University of Amsterdam and the Delta Institute of Theoretical Physics, thinks that gravity is not a fundamental force of nature because it's not always there. Instead it's "emergent" – coming into existence from changes in microscopic bits of information in the structure of space time. He famously stated then that "gravity is an illusion." Well, of course gravity is not an illusion in the sense that we know that things fall. Most people, certainly in physics, think we can describe gravity perfectly adequately using Einstein's General Relativity. But it now seems that we can also start from a micro-

scopic formulation where there is no gravity, to begin with, but you can derive it. This is called "emergence."[8]

What I have come to Know is that a miracle is a minuscule change in one or more of life's variables. It can be a slight change in the fuel combustion, the propulsion, or the degree of angle (angel). It can be as meek or as profound as a morning breeze. A miracle is a change in a life's trajectory. The key here is to observe the subtle shifts and to allow the course corrective maneuvering to get you to your original "Go/No Go" alignment with your Creator, or your return to balance.

To recognize miracles, we must first drop the "Newtonian Illusion" of cause and effect, i.e. "I did this or that so I will receive this or that." A miracle is the knowing or remembrance that you are the miracle. You are an integral part of the miraculous never-ending, never-beginning Creator, or what I call the OMINIVERSE.

Walk like a miracle, talk like a miracle, share like a miracle. Be the miracle in others' lives. Then watch in awe and wonder of what you begin to notice. A million gazillion miracles are happening all around you, and you are one of them!

1st Red Ray, May the Power of God be with you.

---

[8]https://bigthink.com/paul-ratner/remarkable-new-theory-says-theres-no-gravity-no-dark-matter-and-einstein-was-wrong

IV | THE PROCESS

CHAPTER FOURTEEN

The Truth of God

Newton's laws of motion, seen through a new perspective, provide a roadmap to disarming the Universal Gravity Code.

Law #1 - The Law of Inertia

An object at rest or in a state of uniform motion will remain at rest or in uniform motion, unless acted upon by a net external force.

This is also known as the law of inertia. Inertial motion is a motion with the constant velocity. Thus, a force always produces a change in velocity, or, in other words, and acceleration.[9]

The programming of the Universal Gravity Code will continue in its existing state of rest or uniform motion, unless that state is changed by an external force. An unrecognized gravity code will have a tendency to do nothing or to remain unchanged. The veil of unconsciousness is heavy and the code is running without detection. Words to describe the outward appearance of this phenomenon would be: in-

---

[9] https://astro.uchicago.edu/~gnedin/ASTR-BH/PDF/lecture2.pdf

activity, inaction, inactiveness, inertness, passivity, apathy, malaise, stagnation, dullness, enervation, sluggishness, lethargy, languor, languidness, listlessness, torpor, torpidity, idleness, indolence, laziness, sloth and slothfulness.

Law #2 - Coefficient Proportionality

The acceleration of an object is proportional to the net force applied to it. The coefficient of proportionality is called the inertial mass. [10]

When a life circumstance or trigger is introduced, the impact on the Gravity Code will be proportional to the force behind the situation or escalation of the situation. The measure of gravity associated with the new trigger (or the depth of the recognition of the old triggers) also create a proportional response. The assembly of energetic emotions produced produces the inertial mass. Words to describe the outward appearance of this phenomenon would be: triggered, activated, aroused, provoked, incited, motivated, pressed, inflamed, encouraged, irritated, and prompted.

Linear momentum is a very important characteristic of an object in mechanics. It is a product of the object's mass and velocity or, in this context, the degree of the emotional charge. You can think of this as of a measure of inertia. A change in the velocity of which the Gravity Code arises is acceleration: A change in the momentum or energetic force behind the Gravity Code is the force.

In the absence of the net external force the linear momentum of an object is conserved. This is called the law of conservation of mo-

---

[10] *Ibid.*

mentum. It is more general than the law of inertia, because it is a combination of the first and the second Newton's laws.

When the energy behind the circumstance or trigger is equal to the underlying code there will be no momentum. The energetic state of the individual will remain constant.

Law #3 – Action Reaction

For every action, there is an equal and opposite reaction. Example: If object A exerts a force on object B, then object B exerts an equal and opposite force on object A.[11]

The Gravity Code is an assembly of trapped energy within our emotional, energetic and/or physical bodies. The Code has a specific underlying purpose and will present itself when it detects that it is under attack. This so-called attack can be presented as a focused, controlled therapeutic interaction or it can be presented as a re-living of past traumatic experiences. In both cases this interaction awakens the Code, and its reaction to the perceived attack is proportional to the energetic force of the interaction. For example, a gravity code of "I am not enough" based on the initial trauma of childhood abandonment will have a mild reaction to being stood up by a friend for lunch but an explosive reaction to believing they are being rejected by a significant other. Each reaction is proportional to the energetic poke of the circumstance.

I have come to Know that the introduction and allowance of a non-directed, benevolent frequency or energy such as found in The Reconnective Healing Frequency can and will alter the state of any trapped energetic encoding and dismantle the underlying purpose. In the case of "Shit Show," as

---

[11] *Ibid.*

well as many other clients, I have watched distortion patterns known and unknown disentangle and disarm without any direct interaction. There was no need to name, target, touch and/or remember the initial trauma or story. We simply introduced a loving energetic force. The encoding was still there but the energetic pulse seemed to be neutralized. What that means is the client remained aware of the old patterns but had disassociated from the distortions and the story. When we reverse the "cosmological disassociation" we return to the remembrance of our innate perfection and magnificence, of our share in Universal Divinity.

2nd Orange Ray, May the Truth of God be with you.

IV | THE PROCESS

CHAPTER FIFTEEN

---⚜---

The Love of God

There are a million different techniques used on the body, off the body, or through chemistry to help and support with the symptoms of dis-ease brought on by the Gravity Code; unfortunately, for most of us, the sneaky gravity code will then find a new avenue of distortion.

For example, you may have a gravity code of "it is too hard" based on the initial trauma of being disempowered at an early age by an authority figure. In time, you might begin to feel safe in your environment, but then find yourself falling into a binding energetic thought process of excessive worry over possible catastrophic world events. One gravity code loses its grip, but another takes its place. Worry/Fear/Anxiety about *anything* is a distraction from your true essence, one of love and divine peace.

My quest has not been to recognize and understand the gravity codes or to treat the symptoms of their distortions. My purpose, my mission, was to find a way to disarm and dissipate the assembly of trapped energy within our emotional, energetic, and physical bodies. The stories will always remain, but with the de-structuring of the codes, we integrate the light and the dark.

As mentioned earlier, all day, every day for over a year, my internal (and sometimes external) voice was loudly asking the All-Knowing, HOW DO I DISARM THE GRAVITY CODE? Through intense focus, prayer and contemplation, I have come to understand that everything that was given to Isaac (and to many others before and after) has all been pointing at the same answers. I proclaim daily my belief in the omnipotence of The All-Knowing and yet find myself questioning the maladies of this earth plane. Each time I shake my head and wonder why the child starves, the woman cries, the man is at war, the earth suffers, a pandemic arises, I have forgotten my fundamental belief that God the Creator of ALL has implemented a perfect design, a perfect web of intricately placed frequencies, magnetic fields, and universal laws, and has doused it in the most radiant light of unconditional love. This Knowing leaves me to look at a much larger picture.

This is what I have found to be true:

1. God is Love.

2. Everything which exists is made through God and is of God Energy.

3. There is nothing within His creation that does not serve the greater good.

4. I am an aspect of God, an energetic pulse within the whole of the collective consciousness.

5. There is nothing in existence to amplify or diminish the unconditional love of God.

What if there was a frequency that, when introduced to the distortion of the gravity code, could restructure the molecules participating in the binding energy? There is. This frequency or wavelength of information, this energetic pulse, is the pure unconditional love of God. It is the Universal Energy that conducts the orchestra of life and all of its creations. It is God the creator, sharing with His perfect creation. It is the Omniverse!

Knowing all this to be true, I knew there had to be a clue within all of this information to lead me to the Knowing of how to disarm the Gravity Code. Then I heard it: the gravitational pull does not keep us grounded; *gravity pulls the presence of God into our reality.*

When we are dancing in the enlightenment of who we are – "the spark of God" – we are already free. But when we need a reminder or a way to break down the veil of illusion over this plane, we perceive a grave situation, and our gravity codes are activated. The intensity of the activation and the pain it brings will be proportional to the need for a wakeup call.

We have created a system of negative encodings to help us remember the Truth of who we are. The gravity code is not a "bad" thing. The Yellow Ray reminds us of the Love of God. And the Love that is us.

As it says in the Bible and The Course in Miracles, as well as other sacred texts, God is but Love, therefore so am I. Now I see that it is through the relinquishing, the giving up and giving in to love, that we gain all.

3rd Yellow Ray, May the Love of God be with you.

New World Math According to Ginger

Ginger's Whole Number Equation

Emotional Intelligence + Spiritual Intelligence = Clear Critical Thinking

Without emotional intelligence and spiritual intelligence, your thinking will be disconnected and foggy. You will be missing the Critical Component. We are sovereign, sentient spiritual beings using the vehicle of a human body; our emotions are the navigational system, our GPS to our KNOWING in ALL aspects of our life. We cannot disregard any aspect of the equation without skewing the Whole answer.

$$G - \text{God's} \quad P - \text{Presence} \quad S - \text{Sourced}$$

Rearview mirrors are too small to see a full perspective and will only show what has passed us by. Driving a vehicle without side windows or mirrors places you at a disadvantage, for you will not be able to see what is surrounding you or coming your way. The front windshield gives you a glimpse of what's to come. We become better life navigators when we use *all* of our perspectives. Understanding that what is behind us, beside us and before us is never as important or REAL as what is on the road in the exact spot we are right now. Is it a rock, a speed bump, a pothole, an animal, a person, a curve, gravel, or is it smooth pavement? When we stay focused on what IS now, we have a better chance at arriving safe and sound.

I am not whole (vulnerable) ... New belief I am whole and perfect. I AM the opulent white light.

IV | THE PROCESS

CHAPTER SIXTEEN

The Purity of God

I often express my "Ah Ha" moments or Knowings through analogies. My mind and inner knowing will play with an idea for a while, collecting information, ideas, and Knowings until it spills out onto a page.

For several weeks my mind played with the idea of a dry erase board, and then during a quiet moment, the thoughts all came together. You will have to use your imagination to follow along. I promise not to stretch it too far, but I will need your willingness to play.

First, let us imagine that we cover a large wall with that fancy white paint that simulates the surface of a dry erase board. It's great stuff, allowing you to turn any wall in an office space into a "mastermind arena." Now, using blue painter's tape, make a huge rectangle, framing a portion of the freshly painted white surface. What you should see in your mind's eye is a large pristine white wall, and an area on that wall blocked out by a frame of blue tape. Leave at least one foot above and to the sides of your frame and three to four feet below. Get the picture? Great, let's move on. Grab a chunky black dry erase marker and write down the following words inside your imaginary framed area:

ROOT CAUSE, SQUARE ROOT, PLANT, TRAUMA, SHIFT, ZERO POINT, TECHNIQUES, TERMINOLOGY, FEAR, SEEDLING, SEEDED, SEATED, INJURY, ILLNESS, HEALING, ORIGINAL SIN, STARTING POINT, HEALER, ENERGY, FEAR, QUANTUM, PRACTITIONER, PATIENT, CLIENT, TRAINING, WORDS, CRYSTALS, DOWNLOAD, FORMULA, FEAR, BOOKS, STORIES, TESTIMONIES, EFFORT, SEED, PROTECTION, BRAINWAVES, ENCODING, MODALITY, FEAR, TIME, BELIEF SYSTEM. (You may want to add any words that came to mind as you read my words. Trust whatever has come to mind and add it to your vision.)

Perfect. Now, look carefully at your creation, really study it. What if, hiding amongst the words on that wall, is the answer to your personal healing, the healing of others, and the healing of our world. (Now I have your attention!) What if IT has always been right there, right in front of our face? Well, it just might be.

Now take a dry eraser and try and erase your words. Then grab an imaginary bottle of spray stuff that is supposed to help take away the ink. I don't know about you, but in my imagination the words never completely disappear from those dry erase boards; there is a smeary messy grey haze left on the board. Imagine that this grey smeary mess has even gone beyond the boundaries of your blue tape. Ugh, it is soooo frustrating! The spray just dilutes the ink, and the eraser just seems to smear that mess all over. Even when I rub hard, it just spreads and smears, leaving that murky grey haze hiding the pristine white of my original palette.

Did you catch it? Did you sense, know, or imagine the hidden truth?

When I try to find my wholeness within the constraints of this plane of time and space, I end up muddying the waters. My perfection, my magnificence, my perfect balance can only be found when I remember, return, and reconnect to who I truly am. The words are only written on the surface; they did not penetrate the foundation of the white paint. My illness, imbalance, trauma, and illusion of separation have not penetrated my being; it is all riding on the surface, being smeared around and around. I Am the original, pristine, and brilliant white palette of my creator.

So how do we clean up this mess?

The first step is to KNOW what your foundation is: Impermeable Brilliant Pristine White Slate Full of Possibilities and Potential. You are created in the luminous image of your Creator.

Second is to be aware: Perceive that what you are trying, believing, fearing is just muddying your waters, and glazing your foundation with a murky haze. Return your attention to your foundation.

Last but not least, have the right tools: You have the ability to see, feel, and experience who you truly are. You can choose the magic of knowing that your foundation was and has never been affected by the illusion of the murky mess. Focus your attention and reconnect to the purity of who you are, then soak up the veracity of your perfection.

4th Green Ray, May the Purity of God be with you.

IV | THE PROCESS

CHAPTER SEVENTEEN

―――――⚜―――――

The Wisdom of God

And the All that Is has Spoken ... There are many laws governing our existence here in this realm. Be ye focused on the laws of the soul and turn your attention away from the laws of science, physics, and nature. You have come to transform and enlighten your fellow travelers. Be about your work and bring the gifts of Peace to others with your Divine Passion and Sweet essence.

This is another one of my crazy stories ...

Over the past decade of my life, I have uttered the following phrase a million times: "You just can't make this shit up!" I am continually blown away by how my human experience shows me in a BIG way that we are much more than what is evident to our worldly eyes. If you have listened to me speak or if I have had the pleasure of working with you, you know that I am a HUGE proponent of saying YES to our internal guidance system, even when it feels scary, uncertain, impossible or extremely uncomfortable. This story illustrates how one movement (yes) has led to the next moment and on to the next possible movement (yes). It's what I love, love, love about yesses: just one yes leads to many outcomes; it is never a linear event.

A few years ago, I said yes to a volunteer position. I had a strange knowing that this position was going to be offered to me and that I should accept, despite the fact that I'd long ago given up on volunteering for these kinds of positions. I was being asked by my universal guidance system to say yes, so I did. One yes led to another, and by November 2017 a string of events had transpired that made me realize why I had accepted in the first place. I was more than satisfied with that outcome; in fact, I was thrilled. But what happened several months later led to an even greater understanding that nothing is linear, nothing is about one event, one outcome or one yes. It is always an emergence of our life progress.

I was doing what I was supposed to at my monthly volunteer assignment: supporting someone who is leading a group and promoting their individual practice. I set up, break down, greet, and then become invisible for an hour and a half. The fun part is that I get to listen to the group leader and mildly participate in any activities, like guided meditations and so on, though I do so with one eye open because my "job" is ensuring the safety and comfort of the room. In this particular circle, the participants were led to do three different closed-eye meditations (journeys). After mildly participating in the first two, I somehow found myself immersed in the last one. I was gone from that space and on a spiritual journey of my own.

Before I get into the specifics of this vision, I must make a few things clear. First, I want to reiterate that it was unusual for me to go so deep while at work. Second, the vision I had did not go along with how I participate in the Earth's illusion. It involved the Akashic records, which is a place/ topic I do not feel even remotely comfortable discussing.

The Vision

It began with the group leader telling us to go to our Akashic records to access information that we may need in this moment. Instantly, I saw a massive, brilliant white marble building in the sky, kind of sitting in or surrounded by clouds. There was a steep and wide staircase, as wide as the building, leading up to golden doors that seemed to go on forever, reaching up into the sky.

The doors opened as my presence approached (I seemed to be flying, floating or gliding as if on a magic carpet). I checked in with a Being, stating, "Virginia Adams, to see my records please."

She/It nodded and said to a guide who I perceived but did not see, "Take her to room 333-10490249." (I even remember that She/It said the word "dash" after the triple threes!)

I was instantly in a space or a white room (all I know is that at first I did not see anything but white). I said, "I would like to know what I have forgotten," and saw walls of books as high as the sky, vast beyond belief. A booming voice firmly stated, "HAVE YOU FORGOTTEN WHO YOU ARE? You helped tear down this IVORY TOWER!" Then all the books and shelves within that space started to tumble down on top of me, leaving a gaping hole in the ceiling, where there was nothing, or maybe an opening to infinity and beyond.

I was still looking upward, startled and in shock by the voice and what was happening in the space, when I heard the group leader call us back.

I opened my eyes and realized that my consciousness had entirely left that space during the meditation. I was shaking, and my heart was racing. What had I just seen? What in the world had just happened? The leader asked the group if anyone had seen anything. I tried to relay what had just transpired, but I did not have words for the experience.

What does it all mean? I'd be curious to hear your interpretation; in fact, I was tempted to reach out to a physic medium friend of mine for her take on it, but I stopped myself. Though the lessons I have learned thus far in my journey have been varied, they all share one important instruction: I should look within for the answers and then reach out to others for support or confirmation. So I sat with this vision for a few weeks.

Everyone is special, therefore no one is special.

– Dr. Eric Pearl

My interpretation:

The Ivory Tower represents the human tendency to want to prove, show, or be better than, more educated than, more experienced than and more enlightened than. On the other side of the spectrum is to experience unworthiness because of these unfounded comparisons. We see this in the secular world, and unfortunately, this tendency permeates the spiritual or so-called "awakened" world as well. But my Knowing tells me that this is *all* an ILLUSION. There is no-thing that can amplify or diminish my connection and perfection. I AM one with my Creator, even if I have never picked up a book, attended a seminar/training, obtained a degree, or spent thirty years acquiring experience in the art of healing. The only thing that separates any of us from our SUPERNATURAL power is the illusion of separation. All we have to do is remember who we truly are. We are the essence of pure love – nothing more, nothing less. Within that essence is the power to BE whole.

New Understanding:

As mentioned earlier, I do not use the Akashic records in my intuitive work, or at least I don't knowingly do so. Recently I had lunch with another practitioner who is trained in and does use these records, and though we were not directly discussing our intuitive work I found myself positing, "What if we (humanity) were to find out that it is ALL part of the illusion, even our karma and/or Akashic records?" I went on to say that I am coming to a place in my understanding that the concept of karmic past is a linear interpretation of the Multiverse.

"Well," my friend replied with a giggle in her voice, "that would ruin my practice."

The way I see/explore the concept of multiple lives (in my mind's eye) is more like a simultaneous broadcast of side-by-side lives on different stations (you may have heard them referred to as "parallel" lives), with each working on different aspects of our evolution. Now, to add another layer to the crazy craze, I believe we are acting out different personalities/personas in each layered life. In one, I am the abuser, in the other I am the victim; in one I am the hero, in the other I am the villain; and so on, with all lives working towards the Remembrance that we or I have never been separate (because there is no separatism or duality) and on embracing the profound concept of Oneness.

For me, the Akashic records is the Quantum Field, where there is no beginning and no end. The information found there is the "All That IS." Within this Field of ALL there is only ONE Universal Knowledge. The Holy Crap answer, then, is to dissolve (tear down) the concept of separatism and step into our non-duality selves. When I look into your eyes, I know that I am looking into an aspect of Source, which means I am looking into my own eyes. It seems ridiculously simple, right?

So I stand here today and ask you, is there anything in the records of your soul's journey that can help you KNOW that you are ONE with your Creator? Is there any past pain or suffering that will lead you to your KNOWING that you are and have always been PERFECT and that the illusion of this world, with all its wounds, would only have you forget this? Tear down the walls of illusion, "The Ivory Tower," and step into the vast space of expansion where you do not need to figure out or fix anything. You just simply need to remember. It's time to WAKE UP now.

5th Blue Ray, May the Wisdom of God be with you.

IV | THE PROCESS

CHAPTER EIGHTEEN

The Freedom of God: Allow – Surrender – Relinquish

It all began with a simple/complex question. What is the difference between Allow and Surrender? My dear friend and colleague responded with a beautiful and colorful description of Allow as the polite lady and Surrender as the warrior.

So often, in my experience, words or ideas are planted into my psyche for germination. I have concluded that my muse, team of guides, or simply my inner knowing will throw something out into my awareness for me to cultivate into a knowing, which then usually develops into a creative process. I play with an idea over and over again in my head until – poof! – a Knowing comes through, and I write.

While in the process of writing this section of the book, I had placed myself in a self-imposed "state of stuck." Within this space, the words Allow, Surrender, and Relinquish were spinning in my head.

I am well-acquainted with the idea of allowing. It is the exquisite space I enter when facilitating energy healing sessions with the frequencies of Reconnective Healing, or while in what I refer to as the "crystal box of meditation." In both cases, I experience the "tickly" space of "let go." The concept of surrender is also a familiar one; it always brings to mind a twelve-step program, as in surrendering to our Higher Power or to cease resistance to the will of God.

Relinquish, however, was a new word or concept for me, one that required much exploration.

Knowing that Source speaks through many channels, I sometimes ask others for their thoughts while I'm mulling over an idea. And so it came to pass that I posed the question, "What is the difference between Allow and Surrender?" at my monthly Gratitude Circle. I knew that my Source intended for me to ask Melanie specifically and, indeed, once the question left my lips the creative magic of *allowing* began. The visual images Melanie conjured up, along with her beautiful words (and a few new characters to guide me) led to the writing of this section.

These words and ideas come with a caveat: all action words have a negative and a positive energetic pull, just like a magnet, and if you're not careful, your ego might create a negative connotation for them.

Just for today, I ask that you allow yourself to stick with the positive charge.

When combined, the words Allow, Surrender, and Relinquish become the keys to the totality of the perfect energetic flow of life. They are the portal to your connection to All That Is and the equation of unconditional love of self.

Allow

The Polite Outer Lady

Permission Given

Allow is the external display of submission
and loving-kindness.

Surrender

The Warrior Inner Child

Letting Go of Control

Surrender is the conqueror of the illusion of the need to
control. Surrender is the embodiment and the comingling of
both aspects of self – the light and the shadow.

<u>Relinquish</u>

The Wise, All-Encompassing Crone

Accepting the Unknown Outcome

Relinquish is the obedient servant of unconditional love. Relinquish is the embracing of the deep knowing that all outcomes are in perfect order with "All that Is" and the remembrance that we are the Omniverse.

6th Indigo Ray, May the Freedom of God be with you.

IV | THE PROCESS

CHAPTER NINETEEN

The Peace of God

"The higher state of consciousness is somewhere in between the waking, sleeping and dreaming states. Here, we know we "are" but we don't know "where" we are. This knowledge that I "am," but I don't know "where" I am or "what" I am, is called Shiva. This state gives the deepest possible rest that one can experience. And one can achieve this through meditation."

-Sri Sri Ravi Shankar, HuffPost

Prayer

There are times when I meditate, pray, sit in silence or quiet contemplation that I (my essence) seems to leave the constraints of our four-dimensional worlds. What I mean is that I lose my awareness of time and space. I call this my "crystal box," while others have referred to it as being "In the Gap" or a "State of Quiescence." Where were we, really? Or, better asked, *Where was our attention?*

Whenever I describe my crystal box the two words that come to mind are "pristine" and "clarity." While in this state

I am unaware of the sounds and visual aspects of our world, as well as the physical sensations of my body and the chatter of my mind. It's as if I'm enclosed in a crystal box of protection, though that isn't exactly right either because this "enclosure" is expansive and unlimited. At times I might only experience this state for a fleeting moment, but within that moment is eternity.

Once, while in the crystal box, I asked, *Where is this?*

The Knowing that came to me is that this "anti-space" is our true essence. This state of being is where we are all connected, and we are all one. This space is a vast empty ocean of no-where, which is full of love, knowledge, and peace. For me, it is HOME. I believe this is where we all come from or where we exist outside of the constraints of our physical experience; it is the space of Oneness and connection to Source Energy. I also understood that I do not step out of or leave my essence to join this Oneness, rather, I step *into* myself. This infinite space is "within" me, not in the "without" me. Ha, I love that! Oneness cannot be obtained "without" me or you, for that matter.

As I posed my question, I knew in a blink of an eye that when I drop the illusion of my body and this world, I am able to step into the quintessential knowing of what I call God. I saw, felt, experienced my essence joining in the molecules of light, which comprise the personification of God. At that moment, I knew that I was a particle of my Source, a flicker of light that shone brightly along with ALL flickers. My Knowing showed me that together, our flickers create the magnitude of the brilliance of our Source. I stepped out of the illusion of my singularity and reunited (reconnected) to the magnitude of our Oneness.

While on vacation, in November 2015, I received an energy healing known as a Reconnective Healing. I did not know what to expect and really had no perceived reason to do so. That single healing session sent me on a quest to discover the origin of this modality and to ultimately become a practitioner. I began by reading *The Reconnection - Heal Others Heal Yourself,* by Dr. Eric Pearl. As my awareness of these frequencies increased, my ability to enter into a state of being "In the Gap" or a "State of Quiescence" increased.

In 2013, Gary Schwartz, Ph.D., former Director of University of Arizona's Human Energy Systems Laboratory and Dr. Ann Baldwin, Ph.D., of the Laboratory for Advances in Consciousness and Health at the University of Arizona conducted a study comparing the heartrate and heartrate variability of Reconnective Healing Practitioners with people in meditation, Qi Gong grand masters, Reiki masters and marshal artists.

They found that during sessions, both the Reconnective Healing Practitioners and their subjects go into dramatically enhanced healing states. The practitioner experiences a state in which marked and significant brain and heart activity occurs. This state, called "emotional quiescence," is associated with extreme awareness, feelings of peace, connection to the universal energy field, and the ability to perceive on enhanced levels. This far exceeds any the state that is typically seen with other energy healing modalities. It is in fact a very different state from that which has been seen in yoga, meditation, Reiki or any energy healing. This documents clear evidence the Reconnective Healing is something new and different from what has been on the planet before now.[12]

Over the past several years, I have become accustomed to placing my attention on the frequencies of Reconnective

---

[12] www.thereconection.com

Healing during my prayer and meditation time. The connection and healing effects have been immense. My dear friend and mentor Mary Beth Kennedy states it well: "This state is attainable through various meditation techniques as well. Certain traditions allow for the ease of this more simply than others. It depends on which path of 'Golden Breadcrumbs' you choose to follow, which one beckons to you. There is no right or wrong … or perhaps there is no wrong, just right."

Intentional ART

When we intentionally create art, or anything for that matter, we encode/infuse the work with a vibration or frequency. This has sometimes been derogatorily referred to as "bewitching" or putting a spell on it, when the truth is, we are merely infusing the frequency of LOVE into what appears to be an inanimate object. I have come to Know that everything is energy. During the creation of intentional art, we co-create with Source energy. The work created belongs to eternity and all. We are one, and we are love.

Intentional art can be gardening, music, vocals, cooking, baking, playing in the sand, swinging on a swing, dancing, knitting, building a car, coloring, yoga, meditation, laughing; anything where we let go and allow LOVE to infuse our actions. Sometimes there is an end product to remind us and others of the magic or the oneness with Source, and other times merely the vibration or frequency is left. In either case, the result is creating more LOVE, which dismantles the Gravity Code.

Gathering of "Like Hearts"

When several beings sit on points in a plane where their point is equally important to the wholeness of the group, a sacred circle is formed. In this environment, a constant is created. In that perpetual atmosphere of perfect support and security. While participating in sacred circle I have witnessed great things happen. I am always in awe of the deep transformative energy that a group takes on as each individual allows themselves to sit authentically with the support of others. No end, no beginning, just a continuation of love.

Return to Balance

There is something to be said about finding and maintaining balance in your life. The only way I know how to do this is to intently listen to my body and emotions. I even ask them what they need when they are screaming for attention like a two-year-old toddler. Cultivating a relationship with yourself on all levels is crucial to your ability to create balance in your life. You do so by asking the questions, intently listening to the answers, and then taking action. This is where the concept of self-care comes into play. If your body is saying "slow down," you are asked to honor that internal wisdom and do so. Disassociate from the illusion of this world that may be telling you to keep going, push through, or to not be "lazy." A lazy day of self-care is one of the most powerful things you can do. Self-care is a means of realigning yourself to your divinity and returning to balance.

Re-Alignment Assignment:

How do we return to the remembrance of the veracity of who we are? Abraham (channeled by Esther Hicks) says we do so by "changing the disc" we're riding on. By adjusting where our focus is (i.e. moving to a higher-flying disc), we change what our experience is. It is that simple. The more you practice focusing on JOY, the more JOY will show up. The cool thing about Joy is that she always brings along her friends, wellbeing, balance and abundance.

Your re-alignment assignment is based on a wonderful Instagram post by The Reconnection. My Inner Knowing saw this post as "I AM that I am" statements. I have come to Know that I can insert anything I want to create into the "that" of the proclamation. The image below reflects the vision I saw when I read the Instagram post, with an arrow pointing to our Creator, or God. I said, "I AM 'KNOW' I am," and used the post's words but reversed the image and added what I saw.

Make your own list, your arrow of JOY, which will lead you to your source and the remembrance of your innate wholeness, perfection, and magnificence. Go ahead – do it now and go out and play with Joy, for there is no time *but* the present!

7th Violet Ray, May the Peace of God be with you.

19 | THE PEACE OF GOD

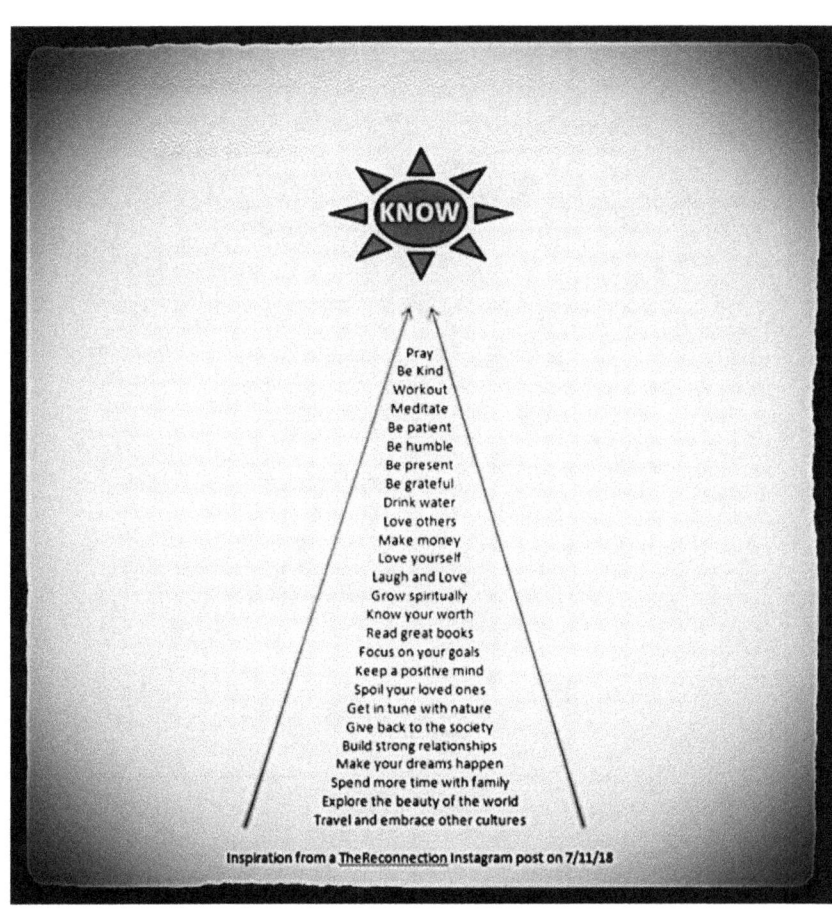

Fill in your words:

_____
_____
_____
_____
_____
_____
_____
_____
_____

CONCLUSION

Joy

> In the beginning, was the Word, and the Word was with God, and the Word was God.
>
> - John 1:1

At this point, you have "consumed" more than thirty thousand words from this book, meaning you have ingested the vibrational content of every word. Just as thoughts have a vibrational component, so do words. In the Christian tradition, they refer to Jesus as being the Word of God. The way that my Knowing understands this is that Jesus, and other Ascended Masters, are avatars, or expressions of God.

As I mentioned earlier, words can have a negative or positive energetic charge, or pull, to them. It is essential to understand the baggage or weight you are subscribing to a word or a group of words. For example, I have used words like Gravity, Alchemy, Disassociation, Narcissism, Relinquish, Surrender, and Death with positive connotations, or what I refer to as having a positive, energetic pull. However, each of these words can also be used to express extremely grave ideologies or thoughts. I ask you now to ponder how the simple application can reverse the meaning of words or their energetic charge within a given context. It is by choice, plain and simple. We, the wielder of words, thoughts, and the power behind them, choose the energetic impulse imitating from those words. You create your reality with the visions, feelings, and ideas that you subscribe to each word that passes through your mind or lips.

As we choose the path of self-love, self-care, and self-forgiveness, we bring all the fragmented characters of self back into alignment. The disassociation which has plagued our existence on this earth plane will dissolve as these aspects of our true essence join together. We will embody the wisdom or our higher-self, the energetic pulse of our emotional self, the lessons of our shadow self, the understanding of our logical self, the guidance of our physical self, and the hidden nuances of our unconscious self into one balanced container. When we do we will come to the Knowledge that it is through our energetic imprint, comprised of all our thoughts and words, that we create our world. Our "Grand Illusion" is just that, a creative work of art. Some of our art is composed of gloom and doom, and other art is rainbow and butterflies. We choose!

CONCLUSION: JOY

Every time we step into a life on this earth plane, be it simultaneous or consecutive, we are given a blank slate. The only component is our true essence, the tiny flicker of light we share with the Omniverse. We then begin creating. When we forget our true nature, we use the mighty force of Gravity to attract God's essence back into our awareness so that we can remember the only thing that exists, the only thing that matters now and forever is our connection to the holy wholeness of the Omniverse. We surrender to the love of our Creator, collapse the constraints of our time-space continuum, and rise to new levels of love. It is through our deliberate disassociation from the definition or limitations of this reality that we are drawn into our God presence.

I have come to Know that any attempt that I make in the expansion of self-love, where I become the witness of my emotional encodings and embrace their effects with self-care, I will have a direct impact on the other beings in my life. I will go as far as to say that my self-love "work" has a direct effect on the illusion of the entirety of our earthly existence. As I embrace and embody each of the aspects of God shown to me through the Seven Rays, I am altering the intricate entanglement with my loved ones and with the collective consciousness at large. How can that be? Quantum Physics has enlightened us on the idea that every action affects the whole; therefore, if I disentangle my emotional encoding and diffuse the disparaging effects on my mind, body, and spirit, I do so for All. I have seen proof of this, albeit on a smaller scale, in my immediate family. As I "healed" the impact of the wounds of my childhood and the abusive relationships of my early adult years, my children began to heal. This, despite the fact that they knew nothing of my "work," nor were they part of it; I was merely focusing on unconditional self-love, and as the effects of my encoding unraveled so did theirs. Knowing this, I can boldly proclaim that as more and more beings turn to unconditional self-love and embody the essence of our divinity, we will usher in global enlightenment.

This brought to mind another question: *Now what? What do we do with the information gifted to us through this book and the energetic imprint contained in the words of its pages?*

Gravity teaches us that it is through the recognition, acceptance, and honoring of our shadow self that we find the light of wholeness. Follow the guidance of the Seven Rays and the expression of the Omni Luminescence. Color your world and raise your energetic vibration to match theirs. Remember your authentic essence and become the power, the truth, the love, the purity, the wisdom, the freedom, and the peace of God. It is time to reverse the energetic charge of your stories and traumas, it is time to rewrite your story, and it is time to introduce the Life Force Energy via unconditional love into every cell of your body, mind, and spirit.

It is time to Wake Up to Your Perfection and Magnificence.

The Beginning of the End

Point A to Point B: The Shortest Distance to Our Evolution

It was Greek mathematician Archimedes (288-212 BC) who first stated that the shortest distance between two points is a straight line. Going around the bend or following a line with a curved detour extends the distance. This does not just apply to physical movement, but to spiritual movement as well; simply put, you have to go straight through the abyss to know the totality of self. Let gravity be your teacher.

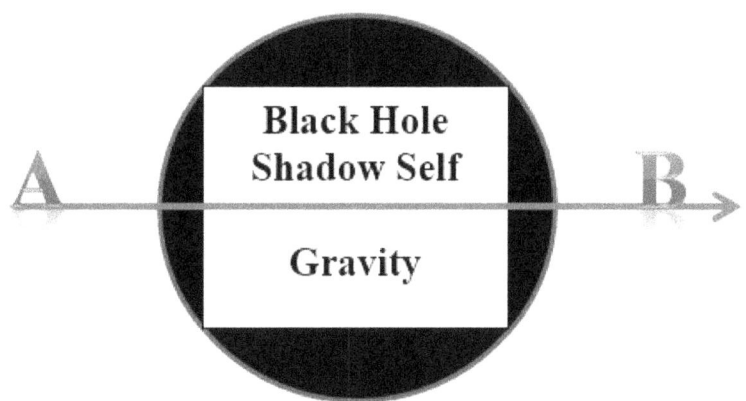

May the Power of God be with you.

May the Truth of God be with you.

May the Love of God be with you.

May the Purity of God be with you.

May the Wisdom of God be with you.

May the Freedom of God be with you.

May the Peace of God be with you.

EPILOGUE

The Grand Celebration

The Grand Celebration has commenced. Beings from near and far, and adorned in their most elegant attire of pristine luminescent white, have assembled in the gathering hall for an event so regal its equal has never before been seen in the Multiverse. There are no words from any language to express or convey the opulence of this space.

The compelling, effervescent celebratory verve is contagious and grows with the arrival of each new being. Brilliant joy and radiant love fill every light body as they step into the hall. With each passing nanosecond, the anticipation of the arrival of the Presence heightens. No words are spoken here, just the roaring hum of a gazillion sweet voices as they breathe out the sound of AHHHHH, the sound of God. The vibration of this roar reverberates throughout the galaxies out into the Universe and expanding to encompass the Multiverse. The vibration beckons all to join in the Awakening of a new era. The wave is proclaiming the arrival of the beginning of the end and the end to the beginning. The Remembrance is upon us.

As each soul arrives, immersing their essence into the collective awareness or the quintessential Knowing of the Presence, they experience their spirit joining in the molecules of light, which comprise the personification of the Presence. Each vibrating as a holy particle of Source, the flicker of light that shines brightly along with ALL flickers. The end of the illusion of singularity in all dimensions is collapsing. All light is now reconnecting to the magnitude of our Oneness.

The Presence's arrival is imminent now; the intensity of the light grows and grows as each being joins its light to the whole. All light beings are drawn to the center by an intense gravitational pull, the pull of the Almighty. As each being is drawn closer and closer to the center of the gathering hall, their essence begins to glow with a brilliance never witnessed before. The light of all beings comingle, and separation is no longer visible. They have become ONE light, ONE voice, ONE essence, ONE Omniverse.

Suddenly, there is a cosmic burst of light of super atomic proportions, and ALL is consumed, leaving a single flickering light, with complete darkness surrounding.

The Presence asks, "Now, what shall We create?"

AUTHOR'S NOTES

Iahhel

The name of Iahhel came to me the first night I sat to write the whimsical Isaac Newton story. I don't recall ever hearing that name or anything at all about this Angel, yet I distinctly heard "Ia-Hal." A Google search revealed the following, and of course it was PERFECT.

Iahhel, Angel of Knowledge, is the patron angel of the desire to know, which is why he has been known to guide philosophers and those who are attracted to mysteries. He fills us with positive and constructive ideas and thoughts, and allows us to rediscover the knowledge we already possess but have forgotten long ago. Iahhel brings enlightenment, wisdom and responsibility, and when he is present in our life, we feel solitude, tranquility, modesty and gentleness. Iahhel is also linked to the payment of karmic debts, so pray for his guidance when you want to discover or get rid of your karma. Iahhel is very helpful for those who have spiritual gifts, including "the claires" such as clairvoyance, clairaudience or clairsentience, and can help anyone connect to their inner self. He likes art, poetry and everything that is beautiful, and can help you transform your home into a place full of positive energy and harmony.

For more information go to https://spiritualexperience.eu/guardian-angel-iahhel/

Number 353

The same night, as I wrote the Isaac story, I typed, "The seal of tau will not be open for another 353 years." It just came out that way. A few months later I realized that from 1666 (the year Newton was in isolation due to the plague and when he penned the secret diary entry I quoted earlier) to 2019, it would be 353 years. This knowledge shut me down. It was the summer of 2018, which meant I had a fast-approaching deadline for this piece of work. Mind you, I had no idea where it was going, what its purpose was, or if it would ever make it to print.

Seven Rays of Light

As the Whimsical Story of Sir Isaac Newton unfolded, I was told during a meditation that the "Crucial Experiment" was the key. I had researched and read about Isaac's life and experiments and it seemed that particular experiment wasn't all that important. I thought that maybe it was just a way to elaborate on the "what if" story, specifically how the angel would appear. Then I was given a vision of the light of the angel refracting into the colors of the rainbow or into rays of colored light. As this vision ended, I was left with the sense of Knowing that it had something to do with the Seven Rays, which esoteric and mystical teachings have referred to down through the ages. I had never paid much attention to these teachings so I decided to do a little research. I discovered that each ray depicted an aspect of God's essence. Poof! Now I understood what was meant when I heard that the Crucial Experiment was key.

π - Pi

Last September, while I was sitting at my computer tweaking a few of the mathematical equations for "New World Math According to Ginger," I distinctly heard a voice in my head say, *Go outside and look at the sky.* When I did so, I laughed out loud. "Pi in the sky," I said, and that voice replied, "Know that your ideas, your dreams, your yearnings to create are divinely inspired." Awestruck by the incredible visual accompanying this message, I snapped a photo (below) and sent it to my daughter Christina. She didn't see the Pi sign, but heard the voice in her head say, "What's the thing about pies?" This was a beautiful confirmation of my "out-sanity" (my new word for the crazy beautiful messages I get). I believe that what is given to me is given to all, so whenever possible, I have been trying to share with others when I get a *woohoo!* message. With this in mind, I posted my message on Instagram, along with the photo. Shortly after, I received a second confirmation from my niece Allison, who lives on the West Coast. "I woke up this morning," she wrote, "and while still lying in bed I connected and asked what it was that I needed to hear. I heard 'pie in the sky' and thought, oh what gibberish … Seeing this post moments later is blowing my mind …knowing that my yearning to create is divinely inspired means so much to me. I have been going in a new direction, focusing on art, poems, and writing, and wondering if I should be spending all of my time doing these things. It's like they are exploding out of me." Woooo Hoooo, Allison's internal voices are the same internal voices as mine. You just can't make this shit up!

The Symbol of Tau

τ

During a meditation, I was told to use the symbol tau. I had NO idea what a tau symbol was or why I would be told to use it. In the strictest definition, this symbol is a representation of the nineteenth letter of the Greek alphabet with a numerical vibration of 300. As I did my research, I understood my muse's request. I laughed out loud when I saw one entry that read, "Tau is better than Pi" (τ > π). I also found the following blog post[13] on the subject:

> *The tau symbol has been used throughout the ages, and it now has a deep significance for me. For example, this symbol was shown to represent the crucifix in many European and Western religious traditions. It was also thought to symbolize a phallus in ancient Egypt and also believed to be a marker for holy waters. We find this image in primitive/native man glyphs as a representation of the meeting place between earth and sky (horizon). Mythology suggests*

---

[13] https://www.symbolic-meanings.com/2007/11/07/tau-symbol-meaning/

this symbol is associated with the Roman god Mithras & Greek Attis. Kabbalistic references indicate the symbol holds to the mystical references of the <u>number three</u> and holds meanings such as: Creativity, Expansion, Magic and Intuition. More literal focus on the Tau reveals its correspondence with the 22nd letter of the Hebrew alphabet & corresponds with Saturn. The symbology of the Templar/Freemasons/Rosicrucian indicates the Tau represents the One God and its three attributes which are: Wisdom, Strength, Harmony. The Tau is found in center circle of the Rosy Croix (rosy cross) – symbolizing the union of the subjective and objective – mysticism and the alchemical practice of the Great Work.

Greater than or less than

When we perceive anyone or anything being "greater than" or "less than," we contribute to the delusion of a world out of balance, as well as the creation of seeds of unworthiness and the encoding of a Gravity Code Loop.

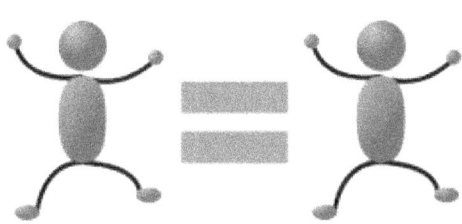

Square ONEness or ONEness Squared. Me x Me (my awareness of our connection) = ONE.

The Circle of Love

When several beings sit on points in a plane where their point is equally important to the wholeness of the group a sacred circle is formed. In this environment a constant is created. In that perpetual atmosphere of perfect support and security I have witnessed great things happen. While participating in the perfection of a sacred circle, I am always in awe of the deep transformative energy that a group takes on as each individual allows themselves to sit authentically with the support of others. No end no beginning just a continuation of love.

ABOUT THE AUTHOR

Virginia "Ginger" Adams is an author, Master Energy Healer, clairvoyant, intuitive mentor, and intuitive artist. She is also a well-known motivator and medical practice administrator, whose dedication, integrity, and intuitive nature have positively impacted many individuals and healthcare practices around the world.

Years ago, Virginia, who had always thought of herself as a practical and methodical person, received a divine mandate to "Heal the Healer." The seed planted by that mandate sent her on a path of discovery, ultimately leading to the opening of her energy healthcare practice.

Virginia has been given the beautiful gift of bringing light and love into people's lives. Her ability to hold a sacred space for another is quite powerful. Be it in a Spiritual Workshop, Intuitive Mentoring Session or Energy Healing Session, clients are benefited by her ability to stand in unconditional Love which transcends in such a gentle way and opens doors to their own vulnerability. Virginia is trained in multiple energy healing modalities but currently chooses to focus her attention on the Reconnection Healing Frequencies which she believes allows for a purer more intense healing session.

What is brought through the Reconnective frequencies during a session is energy, light and information. For each of us that represents something different. It is Virginia's belief that our physical, emotional and spiritual needs are so complex and so varied that it would be impossible for her to "direct" a session.

Clients often feel an instant connection to a deep space of peace. It has been described as being blanketed in Love or embraced by God. This is the space where individuals find their own power and connection and where the healing begins. The power to heal ourselves lies within our innate perfection and our oneness with the universe. Reconnective Healing taps you into this deep reservoir of pure Love where spiritual, emotional and physical healing reside.

To learn more about Virginia and her work, visit www.Virginia-Adams.com.

But wait ...
There's more!

Of course, I wouldn't leave you hanging after such a powerful ride of self-discovery. I would be honored to hear about your journey into the Universal Gravity Code. Please take a moment to send me your thoughts, comments, and illuminations. As a "thank you," I will send a link to an extraordinary guided meditation I made just for you, a graduate of "Iahhel's School of Light." You won't want to miss out on this powerful tool to enhance your journey of self-discovery.

Free Guided Meditation Download

Contact me at https://www.vaadamsenterprises.com/reviews, and leave a few words. I will be sure to send your MP3 copy as soon as I receive your request.

I would also like to extend my other services to you. If you enjoyed the interactions contained in this book and would like support on continuing your journey, I have a few options for you.

- To schedule an ENERGY HEALING SESSION (in-person or distance) or an INTUITIVE MENTORING SESSION (in-person or remote), go to https://www.virginia-adams.com

- Subscribe to my website to receive my blog AND get first notice of programs, events, webinars, and offers: https://www.virginia-adams.com/subscribe

- Check out my online shop where you can find intuitive art and merchandise: https://www.thesnarkybee.com

As always, I love you with all of my heart,

Virginia Adams
A Legacy of Love

www.ingramcontent.com/pod-product-compliance
Lightning Source LLC
Chambersburg PA
CBHW070303010526
44108CB00039B/1663